# The Spiritual Basis of
# Steiner Education

# THE SPIRITUAL BASIS OF STEINER EDUCATION

Roy Wilkinson

SOPHIA BOOKS
Rudolf Steiner Press
London

Y99

Sophia Books
Rudolf Steiner Press
51 Queen Caroline Street
London W6 9QL

Published by Sophia Books 1996
(Sophia Books is an imprint of Rudolf Steiner Press)

A catalogue record for this book is available from the British Library

ISBN 1 85584 065 0

Cover by Andrew Morgan. Photograph by Barry McGlone
Typeset by DP Photosetting, Aylesbury, Bucks.
Printed and bound in Great Britain by Cromwell Press Limited, Broughton Gifford, Wiltshire

# CONTENTS

|  |  | Page |
|---|---|---|
| Foreword by R.A. Jarman | | 9 |
| 1 | Spiritual Science or Anthroposophy | 13 |
| 2 | A Short History of Steiner Education | 19 |
| 3 | The Organization and Structure of the Steiner School | 24 |
| 4 | Phases of Development: Learning and the Seven-year Rhythm | 35 |
| 5 | One World: The Comprehensive Curriculum | 42 |
| 6 | The Threefold Nature of the Human Being. The Temperaments | 54 |
| 7 | Curriculum Subjects: The Spiritual Background | 59 |
| 8 | Destiny and Karma: Education for Eternity | 80 |
| 9 | Unseen Forces: The Effect of Supersensible Influences | 87 |
| 10 | Nutrition and Education | 100 |
| 11 | The Significance of the Festivals | 108 |
| 12 | Esoteric Development and the Teacher | 115 |
| Appendix: | The Spiritual–scientific View of Evolution | 124 |
| | Christianity: The Cosmic View | 127 |
| A Note on Rudolf Steiner | | 132 |
| Bibliography | | 136 |

## Author's Note

The use of masculine forms does not imply any sexual preference. The author follows the convention that 'he' or 'his' in many contexts includes the 'she' and 'hers'. The word 'man', unless used specifically to denote the male, refers to the human being in general.

The terms WALDORF and STEINER education are used synonymously in this book. For an explanation of the term 'Waldorf' see p. 19.

# FOREWORD

Contained in this book are the fruits of the author's long association with the work of Rudolf Steiner and his 50 years in the educational field. Shining through what he presents here will be perceived a practical idealism of the very kind needed in the modern world if our present civilization is to overcome the serious dangers increasingly besetting it.

One of the aims of the book is to give an account of how that particular form of education known as Waldorf or Rudolf Steiner education has been developing over the last three quarters of a century. Another is to show how children from all kinds of background and in all kinds of schools may benefit from the deep insights into the nature of childhood which readers may gain through thinking further over what is presented here. But the main thrust of the book is to show the relationship between spiritual science and education and to correlate education with other aspects of such science.

That modern civilization is facing serious dangers is obvious to everyone who observes the increase in vandalism and brutality perpetrated in our society both by young people and those not so young. It occurs not only in individuals and in small groups but also on a large scale, as witnessed in tragic conflicts in former Yugoslavia.

Rape and robbery, murder and mutilation, together with many forms of drug addiction, lame and pervert our culture in increasing measure the world over. Attempts to control the distribution of drugs are proving more and more difficult, while the subtler 'psychological drugs' imbibed through viewing advertisements and listening to the sound of diseased music are uncontrolled. Monetary profit in media expansion has become enormous. The effects upon present and especially future generations of the 'Plug-in Drug', described a few years ago in the book of that name by Martin Large and others (Hawthorn Press), are becoming more and more serious.

None of these social cancers can be remedied by legislation. Sterner laws against violence can only produce temporary containment. Greedy financial interests fetter the power of governments, whether it be through vested interests (e.g. armament manufacturers) threatening to withhold party funding, or through television and press threatening politicians with a bad image should any opposition to the social malaises be proposed that is inimical to these big businesses themselves.

In any case, since the state of society is no more than the reflection of the nature of individual human beings, it is not through laws, regulations and ordinances that the social diseases will be overcome. We have to start with the individual human being—the true virgin nature of this being—and educate accordingly. At no time in life is this more possible than with children. But the very diseases suffered by modern social life have crept into the way education at large is organized. The teacher has become required to act partly like a factory worker fashioning his products (the children) according to imposed efficiency norms, and partly like a bureaucrat for whom paperwork and the filling in of forms has become the hallmark of existence at the highest level. Such requirements have become encapsulated in the extraordinary term 'educational excellence'. What on earth have league tables, so-called parents' charters, national curricula, the possession of GCSEs in every conceivable subject, and so on, to do with real education?

*Of course* children's progress needs to be tested; they want it and need it, but not in the complex, one-sided manner developed by some of our educational theorists, for whom what appears in final rigid form on paper, tape or video constitutes the goal of educating. It is what the child learns in himself, for himself and for the sake of his/her fellow human beings that really matters. Little of this can be tested by intellectual procedures. Intellect has been allowed to run riot while its maturer sibling, reason, has been ignored. For human reason knows the values of art and religious experience and of what real scientific endeavour consists. Intellect is an essential human capacity but it can only analyse, divide a whole into more and more parts. Reason can take these parts and rebuild with them, synthesize them into more embracing wholes—but only through its ability to enlist the help of those deeper levels of the essentially human, whence emanate the feelings of the heart and the active morality of hands and feet.

The ills of our society and the ills of our general educational system today sustain and support each other in a way similar to the well-known vicious spiralling of rising wages and prices in economic life. We have recently observed (British Medical Association conference in July 1994) the Bishop of Birmingham's condemnation of unchristian reforms in the National Health Service which treat patients like consumers and cause distress to the large number of doctors who see their profession as a calling.

While medicines and hospital equipment, teaching materials and school equipment are all commodities to be bought and sold, neither the healing work of doctors nor the educating work of teachers can be costed. Their salaries are one thing, the actual increase in health and education in the individuals concerned is quite another. The latter cannot be costed. It is quite wrong to treat either patients or children merely as consumers in the economic sphere.

Probably the greatest attack upon the essentially human in all of us today is that through the human senses, upon which we rely to help us to get to know everything in our lives on earth. It is they who serve our human individuality, and their malfunction can only produce lameness in the outward limb-transmitted deeds of our true selves. Noise is the plague of our culture; we have to make an effort *not* to hear. Chemicals and substitutes produce atrophy in our sense of taste. Tranquillizers subdue our senses of touch and health. The flickering of pictures on cinema and TV screens damage retina and ciliary muscle. Secondhand presentations of nature become preferred, for example, to wandering through sun-awakened meadows, walking silent woodland trails at dusk or up crisp-aired mountain paths beneath star-studded skies.

The true educator, in the times in which we are living, needs to pay detailed attention to therapy. The best therapy of all is an education in which every part of the human being, be it physical, biological, psychological or spiritual, is nurtured according to its own needs, not according to intellectually narrowed theories. For all human needs spring from an impulse towards wholeness. It was this that inspired Rudolf Steiner to initiate the many developments associated with his name. How this inspiring seed has germinated in just one of these fields is set forth in the following pages. The reader will discover that each chapter complements, and is complemented by, every other chapter. Only if he becomes able to acknowledge an all-embracing wholeness in the author's presentation, one which can revivify education and counter the social evils of our age, will the efforts of the author have proved worth while.

R.A. Jarman M.A. (Cantab.)
Former chairman, Rudolf Steiner Schools Fellowship (Great Britain and Ireland) and member of the International Council of Waldorf Schools.

Lecturer and teacher trainer at Emerson College and the University of Plymouth (England), Sunbridge College (USA).

# 1. SPIRITUAL SCIENCE OR ANTHROPOSOPHY

Visitors to Waldorf schools, perhaps prospective parents, are usually very impressed by the happy atmosphere and the prevailing friendly relationship between teachers and pupils. They approve of the kindergarten as soon as they see what care is taken with the decor and the choice of toys. They will probably also see a puppet theatre and a Wendy house, and note the artistically constructed furniture (where this is financially possible). They may, however, be surprised to find children up to 6 years of age still in the Kindergarten and may be even more surprised to learn that no formal education is offered until they have passed this age.

Venturing into other classrooms they see the walls adorned with paintings and drawings done by the pupils and may perceive how art pervades the teaching of so many subjects.

On further investigation they are surprised by the extensive range of subjects in the curriculum, by the fact that one teacher takes main responsibility for a class for eight years, by the daily routine, and by the non-existence of a headmaster or headmistress.

There are very good reasons for all these arrangements and it is to be hoped that the following chapters will add to whatever explanations have already been given by their hosts. However, before entering into such details it is necessary to clarify a matter of general fundamental importance.

The word 'spiritual' is contained in the title of this book and it is therefore obvious that reference will be made to some deeper philosophical background—in this case, spiritual science.

Many people stumble over the word 'spiritual' and even more so over the expression 'spiritual science'— a science that is spiritual is considered a contradiction in terms. However, since Steiner education is based on such a science, an attempt must be made to explain what is meant.

Natural science, with all its great achievements in unlocking the secrets of nature and putting them into use, sees the world only from a material point of view. To complement natural science, to unlock the secrets of existence, another form of knowledge is required, which is only directly attainable by those persons who have developed a special faculty of extended consciousness. This gives access to knowledge of higher worlds, and this knowledge is termed 'spiritual science'. It has social, ethical and religious implications.

As far back as we can trace history—to the Hindus, Zoroastrians, Egyptians, Chaldeans, Greeks, Romans and primitive cultures—all looked to their gods. The Hebrew scriptures begin with the momentous words: 'In the beginning, God created the heaven and the earth'. Catholics, Protestants, Evangelicals, Moslems, all subscribe to the existence of God. Spiritual science, or knowledge of spiritual things, is nothing new.

However, appreciation of the divine, or of spiritual matters, changes from age to age. Today, faith is no longer sufficient. The seeking mind wants to know, wants to understand. There are many 'missionaries' in the world at present offering information and guidance on spiritual matters. But, as far as the writer can judge, the one outstanding personality of modern times who has formulated a science of the spirit in such a way as to suit the modern mind and to be appropriate to the modern age is Rudolf Steiner. His breadth of vision, wisdom and accomplishments beggar description. (A short assessment has been included at the end of this book nevertheless.) To his particular exposition Rudolf Steiner gives the name Anthroposophy. This is how he characterized it:

> The mission of Anthroposophy is to bring truths, new knowledge, not to be pledged to any particular tenets. To ask 'What do Anthroposophists believe?' is nonsense. There is no common dogma. That would make it a sect. The common element is the urge to hear the truth about spiritual things. [Lecture 5, *Reincarnation and Karma*, 5 March 1912, Berlin.]

Beyond the earth are sun, moon, planets, stars. On a clear night we may look up to the magnificent dome of the heavens and, if we are not complete philistines, feelings of wonder will arise within us—of awe, of reverence, of our own apparent insignificance. We may have been told in school that these bright objects fly through space and keep to their tracks by forces of attraction and repulsion, but did anyone ever tell us who provided the original motive power? And by what agency is this perpetual motion sustained?

We appreciate the firm earth on which we stand, the waters which separate the land masses and traverse the continents, the wind and the rain, but do we rightly assume that they are only the result of physical forces?

We contemplate a beautiful landscape with its flowers, plants and trees. The man with even a little poetry in his soul breathes a little deeper and maybe sighs because there is something which he does not grasp. He may have learnt about the way plants draw their nutrients from the soil, how the process of photosynthesis works in the leaves and all the scientific explanations of growth, but is there something beyond his immediate understanding? Life? Whence does it flow?

We see the animals, sentient beings, some obviously very closely related to ourselves, perfect in some respects but limited in others. What is their place in the world order and what is their relationship to man?

And what of ourselves? As soon as a person becomes conscious of himself, questions as to the self arise—questions of destiny, of the purpose of life, of death.

Economics often seem to be the dominating factor in our lives. Are religion and morality merely superstructures?

Such questions may be overshadowed by the stress of daily existence. They may be rejected. They may be suppressed by alcohol or narcotics, but they remain and will certainly surface again, if only in times of personal crisis.

Political problems, economic problems, personal problems, abound in the modern world. Where do we turn to find solutions?

Spiritual science is not a panacea. It cannot solve the world's problems overnight but it can contribute to an understanding of them and disseminate appropriate knowledge. To quote Abraham Lincoln: 'If we would know more where we come from and whither we are going, we would know better what to do and how to do it.'

In this sense spiritual science or Anthroposophy offers a contribution towards answering many questions and solving many problems. For instance: it provides knowledge of the origin and development of the universe far beyond the Big-Bang theory; it explains the evolution of the earth and the nature of man; it gives knowledge of the eternal in the human soul and of its connections with the divine; it describes supersensible realms and beings and man's connection with them; it points to the way ahead for future development.

It also shows how, by making the necessary effort, the gates of the spiritual world can be opened by any person.

It is true that statements about some of its aspects may appear a little strange on first acquaintance, but so does the theorem of Pythagoras to those who have no knowledge of geometry, or, to the lay mind, the fact that two gases combine to form water. There is nothing in spiritual science that cannot be grasped through the concepts and ideas that can be acquired today during life in the physical world. In spite of the frequent use of the word 'spiritual', there is nothing spooky about spiritual science or Anthroposophy.

If the above hymn sounds too exalted, let it be pointed out that Anthroposophy can also be known by its deeds. That is to say that it has applications in practical life which are now recognized all over the world, in medicine, in agriculture, in art, and in education—with which we are here primarily concerned.

As an interesting aside it could be explained that some parents send their children to Waldorf schools because they are Anthroposophists, or nearly so. For some it is a matter of a convenient locality. Others send their children simply because they think the schools are good and the children happy, but they take no further interest in the background. Some parents appreciate the education or the particular school but have a reservation about its anthroposophical basis! It has been known for parents to say that they like the school, but wish it were divorced from certain 'crazy' ideas which they may have garnered, or which a teacher may have expressed.

The Waldorf school and the 'crazy' ideas are, however, inseparable. Waldorf schools would not exist if they were not related to these ideas. That unorthodox views may not be appreciated by some people is understandable. The fact, however, that Waldorf schools are successful educational establishments might give rise to the thought that perhaps the background ideas have some validity after all.

It is to be hoped that this book will provide a little enlightenment.

The following two chapters give an outline of the history and organization of the Waldorf school. These are followed by references to some of the basic aspects of Anthroposophy in connection with education. Other chapters are generally informative. Spiritual science provides background knowledge for the teacher. Such knowledge, and the teacher permeated by such knowledge, is the true spiritual basis of Steiner education.

A man or a woman who is inspired by the thought of a divinely created and sustained world will teach differently from one who embraces the idea that the world has originated from some undefined cosmic explosion. The idea of a God-created human being will produce a different attitude from one which considers the human being as having evolved from some accidental combination of elements.

The teacher who has studied spiritual science, and not only studied it but also practised its implications, will have created a substance within himself that flows over automatically to his pupils. In this instance 'implications' mean the practice of meditations given to teachers in which they affirm the existence of divine helpers and ask for guidance. In meditation they also seek to understand the fundamental being of their pupils.

# 2. A SHORT HISTORY OF STEINER EDUCATION

The name Waldorf really belongs only to the first school of its type, the one founded by Rudolf Steiner in Stuttgart for the children of the workers at the Waldorf-Astoria factory. It has since been adopted as the generic name of schools conducted according to Rudolf Steiner's recommendations. In place of Waldorf some establishments call themselves Rudolf Steiner schools. Others take a distinctive name and add Waldorf or Rudolf Steiner in some connection as a subtitle.

It should also be pointed out that there are Rudolf Steiner schools and homes for maladjusted children and such as need special care. These have their own history and they are all separate entities. Their organization and structure will be different from what is described here, but of course they are based on the same world conception.

Steiner or Waldorf education has been in existence for some 77 years. It dates back to the year 1919, a time of unprecedented chaos in central Europe, following the end of the First World War.

The 1914–18 war ended an epoch and, with the old order destroyed, it opened the way for a new social impulse. A preliminary stirring had already manifested in the French revolution with its cry of *Liberté, Egalité, Fraternité*, but a conscious transformation of these ideals into reality was never achieved.

However, there were a few forward-looking thinkers in Europe in 1918 who took an interest in certain ideas put forward by a writer, lecturer and scholar who seemed as much at home in the sciences as in the arts, who was familiar with all branches of learning, who was able to talk to experts on their own ground and who obviously possessed extraordinary insight and faculties. This was Rudolf Steiner.

In the disastrous circumstances of the post-war social order Rudolf Steiner put forward proposals for a threefold organization of society that echoed the threefold needs of the human being. These could be characterized as follows:

1. To gain the basic material necessities of life
2. To be able to live with fellow men
3. To have freedom of thought.

The idea of liberty, equality and fraternity covers these needs. A suitable and just social order would therefore consist of three parts—one might even think in terms of three assemblies or parliaments—each independent but naturally working co-operatively. One would deal with spiritual and cultural life. This is the sphere of freedom. Another would be concerned with the political/rights dimension—equality before the law. The third would conduct economic life and transcend national boundaries on a brotherly associative basis—fraternity.

These ideas were taken up with special interest in southern Germany, discussed extensively and a movement was made towards their realization. Unfortunately, it was not strong enough to overcome inflexible and traditional modes of thought and subsequently collapsed. Out of it, however, came Steiner education.

A group of businessmen approached Dr Steiner to ask for guidance on the way forward. Among them was Emil Molt, the managing director of the Waldorf-Astoria cigarette factory in Stuttgart. An enlightened employer, he had already arranged for his workers to receive talks on educational and social matters, the result of an earlier suggestion by Dr Steiner that workers should be informed about how their special role on the production line fitted into the whole process of manufacture.

During discussions the idea was born of educational renaissance. Since one of the tenets of the threefold order is freedom in the spiritual life, the idea of an independent school took root. Emil Molt offered premises and financial assistance if Rudolf Steiner would father such a school for the children of his workers.

Dr Steiner accepted. He recognized that this was a moment of destiny. He recognized that higher powers stood behind an impulse which could revitalize society. He recruited teachers from various walks of life, who for the most part were personally known to him. They were all probably people of exceptional talent and were familiar with his world conception. Teachers were chosen not so much for their academic achievements as for their ability to deal with children and for their willingness to immerse themselves in spiritual-scientific studies of the human being.

The next step was to train teachers, and to this end Dr Steiner gave several preparatory courses.

As a preliminary stage he spoke of esoteric aspects, reminding the would-be teachers to be aware of the readiness of the good spirits to co-operate. In a properly prepared state of mind the teacher would receive strength, courage and light from the divine powers.

(Meditations were given which are available to responsible teachers. See also Chapter 12, 'Esoteric Development and the Teacher'.)

Rudolf Steiner concluded the first course with the following words:

Let us particularly keep before us this thought which shall truly fill our hearts and minds: that bound up with the spiritual movement of the present day are also the spiritual powers that guide the universe. If we believe in these good spiritual powers, then they will be the inspirers of our lives and we shall really be enabled to teach. [*Discussions with Teachers*, 6 September 1919]

With regard to the actual course work, one can only gasp with astonishment at the immense knowledge and learning that Rudolf Steiner possessed and disseminated. He gave a fresh picture of the developing human being, explaining teaching as a living art, as an interplay between teacher and pupils, rejecting dogmas, traditions and formulae.

In all he held 70 conferences with teachers between 1919 and 1924 (he died in 1925). He drafted a curriculum and in September 1919 the school opened with 256 children and 12 teachers.

The difficulties in launching the project must have been enormous. The collapse of economic, social, political and spiritual spheres was total. It was a time of rampant inflation. The children of the war years were not the easiest to deal with. The bureaucracy had to be pacified. In this instance there was no question of choosing a location or pupils. The conditions were given and the school grew out of the immediate need. In many respects improvization was the only way forward.

Although the first pupils were the sons and daughters of the factory workers, very soon other parents wanted to send their children. In a few months numbers had grown to over a thousand and not all applications could be accepted.

The school's fame spread and it was not long before similar schools were founded in other parts of Germany, other European countries and eventually overseas. One of the latest to open its doors is in Japan. In the Second World War the schools in Nazi-occupied territory were closed by order of the authorities, but immediately after the war they reopened with renewed vigour. Today there are some 640 Waldorf schools, nearly 1100 kindergartens and 60 teacher training institutions, in 46 countries.

It was never Dr Steiner's intention to found 'private' schools. The Waldorf school did not come into being as a result of a thought-out, ideal school programme but arose from the necessity and demand of the times and circumstances. It is unfortunate that the word 'Waldorf' has become a label, which relegates it to the ranks of another 'method'. Dr Steiner expressed the hope that the school would serve as a model or as an example. It was his hope that the principles and suggestions would flow into general educational practice.

# 3. THE ORGANIZATION AND STRUCTURE OF THE STEINER SCHOOL

Waldorf or Rudolf Steiner schools are independent, self-governing entities. They will therefore have individual characteristics. No outside body dictates their programme and there is always scope for innovation. Nevertheless, most of them follow—to a great extent—the pattern of the first school. The common factors are the indications given by Rudolf Steiner. The schools vary according to their stage of development, locality, children, availability and capability of staff, and financial support. The following therefore attempts to give a picture of an ideal school. This is a factual description and does not include the philosophical background to which reference will be made later.

In the best meaning of the words the Waldorf school is integrated and comprehensive. It offers a wide curriculum and includes academic, artistic and scientific subjects as well as practical ones.

It follows the principle of giving equal opportunity to all by means of an all-embracing system. It is a community school for all ages (5 to 18 and over) and for all social strata. There are no internal examinations and a co-operative spirit is fostered in the classroom. Each class contains about 30 boys and girls of social mix. There is no cramming and no early specialization. A friendly discipline is maintained. Theoretically the school is open to all, irrespective of the financial status of the parents, assuming there is adequate outside funding. (In some countries the schools are supported by the state, but in others they can only function by charging fees.)

## The Three Departments

The education is graded according to the chronological age of the child and is therefore in keeping with the child's needs. There are three distinct sections, organized to accord with the three phases of child development. Explanations for this arrangement and other features will follow in due course.

1. **Kindergarten, Nursery or Infant School**. This is where the children begin their schooling at the age of 4 or 5 and where they remain until they have turned 6.
2. **The Middle School**. Classes 1 to 8. This contains the children from age 6 to 14 and consists of eight classes.
3. **The Upper School**. Classes 9 to 12 (or 13). Here are the adolescents in the age range 14 to 18 and possibly 19.

The Kindergarten

For the small children in the Kindergarten a happy and harmonious environment is provided. Although we said that schooling begins here, this is not schooling in the sense of applied learning but really an extension of the home. The teacher is not an academician but a motherly soul with a love of children. That is not to say that he or she should not have qualifications, but far more important than diplomas and certificates is the aptitude and understanding to deal with small children.

Sensible and artistic toys and playthings are provided. There is no formal work expected. Children play, sing, act, model, draw and paint, not as instructed by the teacher but in imitation, since this accords with the child's basic urge. Although there is a necessity for guidance and order, children are allowed to be children.

## The Middle School

A very important step in every child's development is signified by the change of teeth. (See Chapter 4, Phases of Development, for further elucidation.)

It is relevant here to point out that Rudolf Steiner did not prescribe a 'method' of education. He emphasized again and again the need for practical activities in the everyday world to proceed from actual facts in that world, facts which are discovered and verified by close observation and experience. He thus suggested an educational 'approach', an observer-type status, from which an effective and suitable way of educating would evolve. He exhorted all teachers to observe children closely because, from that observation, the child itself signals how it should be educated. The way changes, naturally, with age. Prescriptive theory should not be imposed on the curriculum.

The change of teeth, the second dentition, is a major signpost indicating that certain inner processes have been completed and others are now beginning. Puberty marks another stage.

Having achieved this turning-point signified by the change of teeth the child is ready to learn. Now a group of boys and girls aged between 6 and 7 years is consigned to the care of one particular teacher for the next eight years. Thus a close association is formed not only with the teacher but also with classmates, which provides a sense of security and stability. The teacher becomes guide, philosopher and friend. He or she teaches all the main subjects to this class over the next eight years, and possibly other subjects as well.

One of the great advantages of teachers having to take a variety of subjects over a period of eight years is that they themselves can never get stale or repeat their performance. When they come to do their next stint the world has moved on eight years. Much is new and so is the attitude of a new group.

The main subjects are English, Mathematics, Geography, History and the Sciences. Through the fact of their being taken by one person there is the obvious advantage of economy in teaching, since they can be properly co-ordinated. Other subjects are taken by other teachers according to ability and the needs of the curriculum.

The Upper School

When boys and girls reach the age of 14 they can no longer be treated as children. Their minds are expanding; their feeling of independence grows. Up to now the personality of the teacher has been of the greatest importance, but now the adolescents perceive a teacher's weaknesses and they no longer have the same respect. They will, however, accede to his or her knowledge. Thus it is now the time for experts to take over the teaching and dispense with the class teacher. In order though to retain a continuous 'human' connection, a 'guardian' of the class is appointed. The guardian is approachable by any of the pupils on a purely human basis. The class community remains together as a unit.

## Remedial Aid

For children who may require special individual assistance from time to time, a remedial teacher or a remedial class is available.

## Curriculum

No school has a more extensive curriculum. Perhaps the best way of describing it is simply to list the subjects studied, giving a general survey covering the 12 years of schooling. No account is given here of the age or manner in which they are taught.

Basic literary skills

English—(mother tongue), including practice in speaking, appreciation of language, study of native literature

Literature—fairy stories, legends, Old Testament stories, Norse and Greek mythology, the world's great books

Mathematics—all branches

Foreign Languages—usually two, with introduction to the respective literature

Latin, Greek—somewhat neglected in modern times

History—ancient and modern

Geography—world

Art—painting, drawing, clay-modelling, sculpture

Music—singing, recorder-playing, musical appreciation. Individual tuition and instruments where feasible. School choir and orchestra

Science—botany, biology, physics, chemistry, geology, astronomy, optics, anthropology, physiology, nutrition, hygiene, electronics

Handwork—knitting, crocheting, embroidery, doll-making, basketwork, woodwork, copper beating, pottery, bookbinding

Gardening—practical and theoretical

Gymnastics

Eurythmy—an art of movement created by Rudolf Steiner

Religion—non-sectarian

Surveying

First Aid

Shorthand ⎫ These were included in the original curri-
Typewriting ⎭ culum but will now presumably have been superseded by the tape-recorder, word processor and computer

Histories of painting, poetry, music, architecture, religion
Studies of machines and industrial processes.

What is learnt in school is supplemented by visits to
industrial works, mines, etc. A camping holiday and
excursions are arranged.

A Waldorf school does not lay any particular emphasis
on sporting activities. It is considered that what is given in
the subject matter and the general attitude towards art and
ethics is much more character-building than competitive
sport. Games are played for social reasons.

Examinations are looked upon as a necessary evil to meet
state, industrial or university requirements. The curriculum
is modified to meet these and students are prepared for
whatever their needs may be.

## Festivals

The seasonal festivals are celebrated in an appropriate
manner but the school also stages its own festivals.

Once a month there is an assembly for pupils in the
Middle and Upper School when demonstrations of their
work are given. They take the form of choral recitation,
singing, dramatic presentation, and a gymnastics or
eurythmy display.

In midsummer, parents and friends are invited to a
jamboree with fun and games, side-shows, entertainments
and refreshments. A pageant is a popular feature and the
older pupils present a play (in England, usually by Shakespeare).

## Reports

Reports are given at the end of the school year. These are
not stereotyped affairs with the designations A, B, C, etc. for

achievement and effort, but they are a proper assessment of the individual's strengths and weaknesses, successes and failures, written in such a way that the pupil can read the document and not experience any adverse criticism. It contains words of encouragement for the future and—for children in the younger classes—a verse or maxim that epitomizes these. The verse is something to be learned by heart and kept in the memory. Each child speaks his verse before the whole class at regular intervals.

## Administration

The Waldorf school has a collegiate management. That is to say, all teachers are concerned in the running of the school. They are responsible for all aspects, including the financial one, but they seek professional collaborators from outside to advise where necessary. The school has its own qualified bursar. There is no principal and no hierarchy. One or other teacher, or a small group of teachers, is delegated to undertake specific duties, but no distinction of rank is made which affects salaries. These are paid on an agreed equitable basis and there are no differentials in pay on account of qualifications.

An education that aims to give every young person the ability of self-direction and self-responsibility can only be given by educators who are themselves so equipped. Thus every teacher is autonomous within the agreed framework.

A general meeting of all teachers is held once a week, when some special educational theme will be studied. The meeting then discusses individual pupils and any particular problems from whatever source. Teachers share experiences.

There is also an inner cabinet known as the College of Teachers (Faculty in America), consisting of experienced teachers whose task is to take decisions on intimate matters such as engaging new staff and financial affairs. A new teacher may graduate to the cabinet after a successful trial period. It is obvious that such a body can only function properly when there is unity in outlook.

## Teachers

The demands made on a teacher mean that only those dedicated to their work can fulfil their task. At the same time, virtue has its own reward since the teacher himself must be forever engaged in self-education.

Most teachers have a state certificate because the authorities demand it, but they will also have taken a supplementary course in Rudolf Steiner education either as in-training in a school or at one of the Steiner colleges. Where the government does not demand state qualifications for private schools, some teachers may only have taken the Steiner course. A few personalities may have such natural gifts that they are able to step into a classroom without formal training.

## Parents and Teachers

Parents are encouraged to join the Parents Association and to meet from time to time to discuss matters pertaining to the education of their children.

Besides such general meetings every class teacher invites the parents of his or her children to come together once a term to talk over things which may be of individual concern. It provides an opportunity for the teacher to explain what he is doing and why, and to hear the views of the parents.

Each teacher also likes to visit the parents in their homes for more intimate discussions.

There are other occasions when friends and parents are invited to the school, such as school concerts (orchestra or choir), dramatic presentations, or to take an active part in fund-raising events such as the Christmas bazaar.

## Buildings

It is to be hoped that all schools will eventually have their own purpose-built school buildings. At present only a small percentage has them.

Waldorf schools seek to teach their pupils in buildings which are 'schools', not edifices that could equally well be used as offices or warehouses. It is to be hoped that a school building will have some artistic merit as well as being practical. The approach should be welcoming, offering shelter, with a gesture maybe akin to a mother opening her arms. Classrooms in line along corridors remind one of prison cells. A better idea would be to group them around a main area where pupils can meet. Classrooms themselves need not necessarily be cubistic; windows need not be uniformly square.

Aesthetics is a formative force to be taken into consideration not only in the outer design but also in the inner architecture and furniture. Classrooms can be pleasantly coloured and can contain, along with other areas, artistic pictures or artefacts.

A pleasant surrounding environment, with grass, flowers and trees as well as playing areas, is naturally desirable.

## The Daily Round

Lessons begin at 8 or 9 a.m. and there is no general assembly. Each group of children gathers in its respective classroom and each child is greeted individually by the teacher. The session opens with a prayer or suitable verse and is followed by a little social activity, such as singing, choral recitation or recorder-playing.

The Main Lesson follows. (We are not describing the Kindergarten here, which has its own routine.) This is about two hours long; such a time-span allows the pupils to become really absorbed in the subject. Lest anyone still thinks that two hours is too long a period for concentration, it must be emphasized that although the subject is constant, the activities around it are not. Thus part of the time is spent listening to the teacher's exposition, part writing, reading, making illustrations or even acting.

A pause after the Main Lesson is followed by two lessons of approximately three quarters of an hour in the younger classes, the number of lessons increasing with age. Art and practical activities require a double period. A midday break and other pauses are variable and depend on circumstances.

The Main Lesson subject is given in a so-called 'block' period. That is to say, the same subject is dealt with over a period of three or four weeks. The attempt is made to form the material so that it is a complete chapter.

Every effort is made to do the intellectual work in the mornings when minds are fresh, followed by artistic, physical and practical activities in the afternoon. As far as possible, a certain rhythm is established in the sequence of lessons so that the same thing, or something of the same nature, is taken at the same time each day. Of course one should not overtax the brain, so something that is a little relaxing must be included.

Homework is a variable feast. If children have been taught properly and their interest awakened, they will probably be happy to add to their work at home by reading or making illustrations in connection with it. The case is different if examinations are in prospect. Then it may have to be imposed.

## Integration with Vocational Training

Several Waldorf schools in Germany include vocational training in their curriculum. The details are different in the different schools but the main arrangements are approximately as follows.

All pupils receive the regular curriculum up to Class 10, at the age of 16/17. Then there is a division. This may be into two—between those of an academic bent and those more inclined to practical work—or into three, the third being social work. The academics will strive towards the Abitur ('A'-levels, University Entrance Examination or similar), the others towards obtaining qualifications in their respective fields.

In practice, the pupils of Classes 11 and 12 are still kept together as entities and have about half of their lessons together. These include the mother tongue, history, geography, mathematics, physics, chemistry, biology, social studies, history of art, etc., and a foreign language. Art and gymnastics are also practised in common. The pupils then separate to follow their special courses. The schools have their own workshops and facilities where possible. After Class 12 an extra year is added for specialization—to gain the Abitur, certificate of proficiency or similar qualification.

Training for the following professions is possible in some schools (but not all): carpenter, cabinetmaker, fitter, mechanic, lathe operator, gardener, nurse, teacher.

In a few schools there is a greater emphasis on practical work without the specific aim of gaining qualifications.

# 4. PHASES OF DEVELOPMENT: LEARNING AND THE SEVEN-YEAR RHYTHM

In Chapter 3, the three departments of the Waldorf school were described—Kindergarten, Middle and Upper School. Although the school is a unity, there is a very sound reason for this arrangement. It lies in the nature of human development, which has a seven-year cycle. The first two stages and the following adolescent stage are the most notable. The staging posts are the second dentition and puberty.

Spiritual science looks upon child growth as a process of incarnation. A soul-spiritual being unites with the physical body, and the process of growth is one of fusion.

To observe what manifests, what becomes more and more defined in children's features and movements, is to observe how the spirit works through the human form into the physical world. It is a religious experience.

One observes the helplessness of the baby. It lies in its cot, sleeps a great deal and does not take earthly nourishment directly but needs its mother's milk. Not being able to stand means that the spirit has not yet taken sufficient hold of the body. (Adults also lie prone in sleep or in a faint.) Only gradually does the child learn to stand and walk, then speak and become more capable of looking after itself.

A change, mentally and physically, takes place at the age of 6 to 7 and 13 to 14, and again at 21.

In order to understand the process that is taking place it is necessary to consider what spiritual science has to say about the constitution of the human being and his relationship to the other kingdoms of nature.

What is obvious to everyone is that the human being has a physical body, which includes the flesh and bones. The Bible tells us that the Lord God formed man out of the dust of the earth, and we recognize that at death the body disintegrates into this 'dust', i.e. its mineral content.

We see then that the physical body is related to the mineral world, but the mineral world is lifeless and hence it cannot be the builder or sustainer of the form. When a person is alive, his body has a form which is more or less constant. It may change a little with age but it does not grow an extra limb. Bits of it, such as the hair and toe and finger nails, can be cut off but grow again. And provided an injury is not too severe the body restores itself.

There is, therefore, something at work which acts as a restorative. With normal vision we see only the effect, just as we can see trees swaying in the wind without our seeing the wind. People with special gifts may be aware of a sort of second body gently projecting from, and around, the physical. It is called the body of formative forces, or the etheric body. (Although the term 'body' is used, it must not be thought of as material.) Man has this force in common with the plant.

The human being can feel happy or sad, get excited or stay calm, be attracted to the opposite sex, enjoy food and drink or indulge in a thousand and one other emotions. He has instincts and organs of sense perception which call forth a response. It is a state of consciousness. There is therefore a third attribute and this he has in common with the animals. It is known as the astral body.

The fourth principle is the one which raises the human being above the rest of creation. Man stands upright, at least in waking consciousness. He is conscious of his consciousness. He thinks and he can express himself in speech. He possesses a memory, something distinct from what might be called memory in the animal. The animal eats because it is hungry. So does the human being, but he remembers the desire which arose in hunger so that not only the present feeling of hunger drives him to seek food but also the memory of past desire. To some extent he can control his emotions, depending on individual maturity. He does not necessarily follow the pattern of his fellow men. He has a feeling for self, for his own individuality. In addition therefore to a physical, etheric and astral body, he has a force, a faculty, an entity known as the ego. It is a word borrowed from Latin and means 'I'. It is the core element, the eternal spirit.

Of course the baby possesses all these 'bodies' at birth, but in the course of growth their relationship changes—or rather their changing relationship manifests in growth.

At birth the physical body, which has been growing within the mother, becomes free. At the age of 6 to 7 one could speak of a freeing of the etheric, at 14 the astral. The human being is considered mature at 21 when the ego becomes, so to speak, free.

Before birth the child lived in the spiritual world and felt at one with it. The feeling of being at one with the world continues after birth for the first seven years, gradually diminishing. Thus the small child is very susceptible to all that is around it. Its nature is to imitate what takes place in the environment. Children of this age express themselves essentially in will activity.

The coming of the second teeth marks a stage of completion. The pattern of the physical body is laid down. Up to now the inner forces of the child have been working at its physical development and it is therefore educationally unsound to interfere in this process with actual teaching. This is why there is no formal instruction in the Kindergarten of the Waldorf school. Children learn by imitation and example.

Their education depends on what the teacher does, how he or she acts, feels and thinks. Children will copy what is set before them. This also applies to matters that may not be apparent, such as the inner attitude of teachers and even their thoughts and feelings.

A psychological change, together with the physical development of the second teeth, ushers in the second phase. Between the ages of 7 and 14 the child's reaction to the world is quite different. Whereas the will forces appeared particularly active in the first, imitative phase, it is now the feelings which are particularly engaged—and therefore the way in which subjects are presented should stir the emotions. This is achieved by pictorial, imaginative presentation. For instance, in speaking of the character of a tree, is it a dainty lady or a strong old man? In gardening, what is the work of Willy the Worm in providing healthy soil? At the same time children need close contact with a human being to whom they look as an authority—hence the class teacher.

But the manner of presentation is not the only thing to be brought into line with chronological age, there is also the choice of subjects. For instance, the age of 9 or 10 is considered the correct age to introduce grammar and practical subjects such as house building and gardening (in an elementary way) because of children's growing awareness of the outer world at this age.

It is a wonderful and fruitful experience for children aged 10 to make a loaf of bread and realize all that is involved. It can also be a religious experience.

As physical maturity approaches, the teaching of the sciences is appropriate to accord with development or, one could also say, with the stage of incarnation. (These matters are dealt with at some length in the author's book *Commonsense Schooling*.)

After puberty children begin to move into the adult world, and education becomes a matter of appealing to the intellect and independent powers of judgement. It is therefore educationally justified to differentiate between

Middle and Upper School and to put instruction in the latter into the hands of specialists.

At the age of 13 to 14, the child leaves the pictorial sensory domain and is able to combine sensory perception with his own thinking—hence the importance of basic craft skills such as basket weaving, carpentry, copper beating and smithing where possible, besides the academic and artistic work.

Craftwork requires care and individual judgement and decision. The creative urge is stimulated. Not everything turns out as planned but success and failure are necessary experiences.

Throughout the school, class groups remain together. Each group becomes a social community with a life of its own. Learning in groups fosters social understanding. Individual learning is stimulated by mutual interest and assistance.

The adolescent feels more and more the strength of his own incarnating ego, and in a sort of between-state he lives in inner conflict. One sign of this is that, at about the age of 15 or 16, there develops an aversion to painting in watercolours. This is counteracted by switching to black and white drawing—chiaroscura. It is a world of light and darkness demanding careful observation and execution. Charcoal, graphite or even ink can be used. A favourite exercise is to copy Dürer's *Melancholia,* using charcoal, but it has first to be studied with the help of the teacher.

After this interlude a desire for colour and free artistic expression manifests itself again.

As a balance to learning about the sciences, a study period on poetry as an art is offered. Having practised recitation all through the school, pupils have some instinctive appreciation of poetry. Now they should acquire knowledge of language—colloquial, literary and poetic. They learn about rhythm, rhyme, metre, sound, figures of speech and the great works of poetry.

An adolescent's moods swing back and forth; sometimes they are critical, sometimes overbearing. Acting offers a therapy—to be someone else. All sorts of qualities are demanded, such as imagination, bodily command, speech, self-confidence in front of an audience, persistence, memory, enthusiasm. As a project, producing a play is an excellent social exercise, since all must co-operate.

A few notes might be in place here on the further seven-year cycles.

It is a remarkable fact that every seven years the substance of the body is replaced, yet the person inhabiting it remains the same. The cycles continue throughout life and every seven years a sort of spiritual metamorphosis also takes place. They are an important factor in further education, which we could also term spiritual development. In the lecture series *Man as Hieroglyph of the Universe* Rudolf Steiner says that 'to assimilate what has been learnt intellectually about spiritual matters requires seven years. Then it is reborn.'

Every period of seven years witnesses the birth of new faculties. The following indications are aphoristic and apply generally. It is obvious that certain characteristics may appear at any time but they are particularly strong in the periods mentioned.

21–28 Enhanced feeling of self and independence. Motivated by feelings
28–35 Seeks understanding in the light of thinking
35–42 The ego is active in the will. Assumes full responsibility. Vigorous hold on life. Feels properly incarnated
42–49 Self-reliant. Takes initiative. 'Life begins at forty'
49–56 Develops broader horizons and greater perspectives. Two possible directions. More benevolent and gracious or the opposite

56–63 Becomes aware that time is running out. Questions destiny. Retrospective viewing

63–70 Characteristics depend on earlier efforts. Can develop humanitarian ideals or become self-centred. With the right background remains young in spirit

70–77 Fruit of earlier experiences matures. Can be attuned to the divine, inwardly tranquil and at peace, or the opposite

77–85 Readjusts. Revalues. Accepts fate.

# 5. ONE WORLD: THE COMPREHENSIVE CURRICULUM

One of the salient features of the Waldorf school is its all-embracing curriculum, as detailed in Chapter 3. (Reference will be made to specific subjects later.)

Apart from the utilitarian aspects of a good education, one could cite two reasons for such comprehensive cover.

1 It reflects the oneness of the world.
2 It furthers the human being's search for 'self'.

At some time of our lives most of us will have moved house. We would have been aware of a strange feeling of disorientation until we became familiar with our new surroundings. Similarly, and on a larger scale, human beings want to learn about the world around them. But the human being has an innate urge not only to discover the secrets of the material world but to understand his own nature and his own place within the world.

To teach a child only a limited number of subjects means to restrict its mind. Naturally, it is impossible to teach everything and eventually some specialization will be necessary, but that does not alter the fact that pupils can at least be made aware of all fields of knowledge. The giving of knowledge can be looked upon as a sort of food which meets a human need. As the child grows so his consciousness expands, and this natural development is furthered by the choice of subjects offered and the method of presentation.

Furthermore, to teach subjects in compartments, as is often the case, is to develop a piecemeal view whereas life itself demonstrates a complicated, intertwining web. Each subject is but one part of a whole, and for a comprehensive world view it needs to be correlated with others. For instance, if we think of a subject like Geography—the word itself means 'description of the earth'—it is not difficult to see how other subjects can be linked up with it. The earth comprises not only rocks, mountains, plains, rivers and oceans but also plants, animals and human beings. The atmosphere is part of it. Sun, moon and stars belong to it in some measure. The earth's crust contains minerals and a multitude of other useful materials. There are many different nations or peoples on the earth with their different cultures. Some areas of the earth are sites of past great civilizations which have produced great ideas or works of art. One might be wandering now into the realms of history or the development of art, but they are all linked.

## 1. The Oneness of the World

To illustrate the idea of unity, let us consider the following. On the earth nothing can be properly understood if it is looked upon in isolation. Crops are dependent on soil and weather. Worms and animals revitalize the soil. Trees yield food and timber and, together with plants, they regenerate the air we breathe. Our exhaled breath contains a substance which they need. Bees and insects seek out flowers to find their nourishment and pollinate them at the same time.

In recent years ecology and matters of pollution have been very much in the news. It is now realized that cutting down the rain forests interferes with the weather; that spilling factory waste and sewage into the rivers, lakes and oceans poisons them; that the use of artificial fertilizers seeping through the ground pollutes our drinking water; that smoke and gases pumped into the air from our industries and machines produce acid rain which destroys vegetation. It is becoming obvious that a world conscience is required and action on a world scale.

Human beings belong to a tribe, race, nation or community of one sort or another. They are related to one another and interdependent in many ways. The actions of one group affect another—regretfully not always to their mutual advantage. Yet the earth is the home of all mankind and there is but one humanity. This should give thought for social relationships.

The earth itself is one entity in the cosmos among many others. We look into space and see the sun, moon, planets and stars apparently moving around us in constant rhythmic pattern.

No one will dispute the fact that the sun has an effect on the earth. It brings warmth and light. It stimulates plant growth. It even lightens the hearts of the lowly earth-dwelling peoples. In agricultural circles it is accepted that the moon has an effect on plant growth. Certain experiments by Lawrence Edwards and explained in his book *The Vortex of Life* show how planetary influence affects plants and trees (see reading list). The earth's human inhabitants are also subject to extraterrestrial influences as instanced by both ancient and modern spiritual scientific knowledge.

Before elucidating this point we will consider the idea of unity as it applies to the individual person.

Contemplation of the human being can only call forth the highest degree of wonder—this balanced framework, feet on the earth, head held high, arms free to create.

A human being has weight but he himself does not feel it. He has the ability to remain upright when the forces of gravity would pull him to the ground, such as happens when he loses consciousness. There is a power within him that keeps him erect, and this is not of a physical nature.

In his natural upright stance man views the world around him and the heavens above, unlike the animal whose orientation is towards the earth. The bones reveal remarkable feats of construction, providing the greatest strength with the minimum of substance. The way the arms, legs, wrists and ankles move demonstrates genius in mechanics.

Within the body are the various organs—the heart regulating the circulation of the blood, the kidneys purifying it, the lungs taking in the mixed gases of the air, extracting what is required and expelling what is not. Each organ has its own rhythm and its own characteristics, yet they work harmoniously (at least in the healthy person).

Consider what a wonderful process takes place in the matter of digestion. Material foreign to the body is taken into it and worked on in various ways. What is essential for the building up and maintenance of the substance of the organism is extracted and the waste discharged. Consider the self-regulating heating system and the way in which the blood is regenerated to serve the rest of the body.

The physical organization of the human body provides a wonderful example of diversity within unity.

In Chapter 4, we called attention to the fourfold being of man, pointing out that he contains within himself elements of the mineral, plant and animal world, and beyond those an individual essence, the ego. But the human being is also related to the cosmos. Spiritual science records that the universe, earth and man have evolved together (see the Appendix, p. 124) and we should therefore find mutual correspondences. One striking relationship between man and the universe is to be found in their having rhythms in common.

In an external sense we measure our time—days, nights, months—by the apparent movement of sun, stars and planets, but there is a closer connection between human and cosmic rhythms. One of the most obvious is the female menstrual cycle which has a moon rhythm.

We can all observe the passage of sun, moon, planets and stars through the heavens but there is also one which is not so easy to comprehend. This is known as the precession of the equinoxes and it gives a cycle which is known as the Platonic or Cosmic Year.

From the point of view of the earth, the sun and the 12 constellations of the zodiac circle the earth every 24 hours, but the sun and the zodiac have a slightly different rhythm. This means that in the course of a year the sun passes through all 12 signs—hence our 12 months. Every year, in springtime, the sun comes to what is called the vernal equinox, about 21 March, and covers a particular stellar position. Every year the sun slips a little further from this position and after 72 years it is 1° behind it. It takes a period of 25,920 earthly years before the sun once more covers the original position. This is the Platonic or Cosmic Year.

If we share out the Cosmic Year of 25,920 years among the 12 signs of the zodiac, we have a particular relationship of the sun to one sign over a period of 2160 years. This is a time span during which a civilization arises, flourishes and declines.

Taking the figure of 25,920 and dividing it by 24 gives us the equivalent of an hour—a cosmic hour. Divided again by 60 we have the cosmic minute $\frac{25,920}{24 \times 60} = 18$.

Now let us consider a human rhythm. The average number of breaths inhaled and exhaled by the human being is 18 times a minute. In a day that means 25,920 times.

If we divide the cosmic year of 25,920 by the approximate number of days in the year (360), we arrive at the number of our years in the cosmic day, i.e. $\frac{25,920}{360} = 72$. To take the exact figure of 365 would produce a figure slightly lower. This figure reminds us of the life span mentioned in the Bible: 'The days of our years are three score and ten.'

Sleeping and waking are breathing processes. In going to sleep every night and waking in the morning we excarnate and incarnate 25,920 times in a lifetime of approximately 72 years. We are breathed out of the cosmos for a cosmic day before being breathed in again.

Not only do these human and cosmic rhythms coincide,

but the physical structure of the human being is, according to spiritual science, actually a mirror of the universe. Each region of the zodiac can be looked upon as the home of particular spiritual beings and a centre of forces. There are 12 signs of the zodiac and 12 corresponding parts of the human organism. The fact that most of the signs have the name of an animal means that the characteristic forces manifest in these creatures. (Zodiac means 'animal circle'.)

The medieval picture below shows the correlation. Latin and English names are given.

While the forces of the zodiac correspond to the human physical structure, the planets and their forces are mirrored in the internal organs. (In this context, sun and moon are considered as planets. Planet originally meant 'moving' as opposed to 'fixed' stars.) That a connection exists can be shown in the medical field via medicaments processed from the metals which also correspond to the planets. Thus for example:

| Sun | Heart | Aurum (gold) |
| Moon | Genitals | Argentum (silver) |
| Mercury | Lungs | Cinnabar (mercury) |

This is, of course, a very specialized area and the above can only be regarded as mere indications.

The adepts of former times recognized a connection between the planets and the inner organs. They used the names of the planets to designate these. Thus they called the spleen an inner Saturn; the liver, Jupiter; the gall bladder, Mars. The heart was ascribed to the Sun, the genitals to the moon, the kidneys to Venus.

In connection with the relationship of planets with organs and resulting effects, it is interesting to note certain words derived from the planets that refer to human behaviour. Perhaps this is a relic of times when there was more understanding of these matters or when people were more susceptible to these influences.

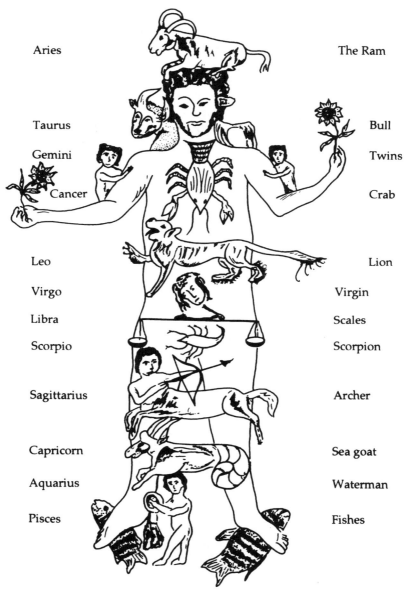

| | |
|---|---|
| Aries | The Ram |
| Taurus | Bull |
| Gemini | Twins |
| Cancer | Crab |
| Leo | Lion |
| Virgo | Virgin |
| Libra | Scales |
| Scorpio | Scorpion |
| Sagittarius | Archer |
| Capricorn | Sea goat |
| Aquarius | Waterman |
| Pisces | Fishes |

(Based on an illustration from *The Evolution of Mankind* by Guenther Wachsmuth, Philosophic-Anthroposophic Press, Dornach, 1961.)

Everyone knows what a 'sunny' nature is. We also speak of a 'jovial' person (Jupiter), a 'mercurial' character, a 'martian' attitude, a 'saturnine' figure. 'Venusian' is rare but 'lunatic' meaning 'moonstruck' is common (*Luna* is the Latin for moon).

Shakespeare, and others, may tell us that our fate is in the stars. So do the astrologers in our popular newspapers, but it has been rightly said that these readings should be read for amusement and not enlightenment. Nevertheless, there is a reality in the horoscope. It shows the forces with which one enters earthly incarnation, but what a person does with them lies in the sphere of his own free will. On this subject Rudolf Steiner writes (*The Spiritual Guidance of Mankind*):

> A certain horoscope is allotted to a person because, within it, those forces find expression which have led him (or her) into being. Thus a man is put into his place within physical existence, and it is in accordance with his horoscope that he guides himself before entering earthly existence.

There are then obvious connections between man and the cosmos in addition to his relationship with the four kingdoms of nature. This fact would support the contention that the human being is a microcosm within the macrocosm. Thus he is related to all things and, to feel at home in his environment, he needs to know it, cosmic as well as terrestrial.

But there is something more. It is obvious that a person's deeds affect his fellow men, women and surroundings. What is not so obvious is how his actions, or even his thoughts, affect supersensible worlds and their inhabitants. If nature, earth and the human being are integrated in the cosmos, what a man does or thinks is then also of consequence to the spiritual world and to the hierarchies, the higher beings who dwell in cosmic space (see Chapter 9).

Natural science has opened out vast vistas and no one

would deny its enormous achievements. It gives us facts and interpretation of facts which are not always easy to dispute. Nevertheless, there is a tendency towards dogmatism and this closes the mind.

The following may illustrate the point.

From our standpoint on earth the planets appear to be small encircling objects of light. Up to the fifteenth century they were considered not just as bright orbs but as whole spheres, centred on earth around whose circumference these visible objects orbited.

Darwin wrote about the descent of man, but his followers deduced from it that monkeys are men's ancestors— accepted at one time, but now questioned.

Not so long ago it was believed that the earth was flat.

Medical science once pronounced that travelling by train would shatter the nervous system. The leech was once the doctor's panacea.

We see that in the course of time science changes its tune. This may give rise to the thought that scientific truth is not final. There are also questions which natural science has not yet answered. For instance, scientific analysis of a plant tells us a great deal about its mineral content but little about its being. Astronomers may tell us that the planets revolve about the sun under forces of mutual attraction and repulsion, but so far they have not told us who or what provided the original impulse.

If we consider explanations of the origin of the universe, we immediately come across a contradiction. Natural science makes no mention of divine activity yet religion would have us believe that heaven and earth are of divine creation and that with regard to the human being 'The Lord God formed man out of the dust of the ground, and breathed into his nostrils the breath of life; and man became a living soul' (Genesis 1).

We return to the matter of the wide curriculum and the idea of unity.

The Waldorf teacher has a difficult task, particularly the science teacher. He accepts as fact that the physical world has a spiritual origin and is permeated by the spirit. Matter is the result of hierarchical activity (see the Appendix, p. 124). The book of nature is a script of the spirit, but such views are not universally held. It is not for the teacher to impose his views on the children. The solution is for the teacher to show the phenomena and give the accepted explanation where necessary, but also point out that it may not be the ultimate truth. This leaves open the possibility of deducing a spiritual background. The teacher could cite Kepler who, when he discovered the laws of planetary movement, accepted their harmony as an expression of divine creative powers. This also afforded satisfaction to his soul.

Obviously wide studies open the mind. If the teacher can convey the idea of oneness, of interdependence, of inter-relationships, it might suggest an overall plan. Such a plan can be perceived by human thought, but who conceived it? The thought might lead to the realm of the divine.

## 2. The Search for 'Self'

The Waldorf school is a school for life. It does not seek to train youth to be bankers, politicians, diplomats, doctors, engineers, artists, clerks, labourers or anything else, but to become human beings. One is reminded of the question put to the little boy and the classic answer:

Question: What would you like to be when you grow up?
Answer: A man.

It is obvious that the basic skills for life on earth must be taught, but in the Waldorf schools education of the whole person is considered primary. Adults need to feel themselves as free human beings, not constrained by being in some situation into which they have been pushed.

Steiner education is not so much concerned with teaching subjects as developing faculties. Physical exercise develops the body; mental and artistic exercise develops mind and soul.

To learn facts, parrotlike, in order to repeat them may strengthen the memory but it does little to enhance the other sides of human nature. The purpose of learning is to develop faculties, and seeds slumbering in the human individual may need to be awakened. Genius will probably break through but if, for instance, a potential musician of modest talent does not have his interest fostered, the probability is that his gift will wither or he feels frustrated.

The teaching of different subjects will develop different faculties. Mathematics will develop logical thinking; Geography, if taught in the comprehensive Waldorf way, will encourage social understanding; Art will develop an aesthetic sense. To be wholly human means to develop all sides of human nature.

Wide interests are an antidote to narrow-mindedness, parochialism, chauvinism, and also maybe to the prevalent spate of violence and crime. Hence another need for a wide curriculum.

There is, however, another point.

From the spiritual world the human being comes into earthly incarnation with certain tendencies, potentialities and ambitions, acquired as a result of experiences in previous existences. In order to find his proper place in this world, he needs to be offered all possibilities of development.

It could therefore be said that the purpose of education is to help the individual to fulfil his karma. (See Chapter 8, Destiny and Karma.) The teacher is an intermediary and his task is to guide the incarnating individualities into the physical world and to equip them for earthly existence, bearing in mind what they bring with them from the past and what they are likely to take with them into the future.

It is also the task of teachers to equip themselves suitably—by studying the laws of child development and such knowledge as spiritual science disseminates. Properly equipped teachers are then in a position to act freely, to observe and introduce into their teaching what is required, as required. (See Chapter 12, Esoteric Development and the Teacher.)

Education can only flourish on the basis of human relationships, of person to person. Diktats from above, regulations, prescriptions, form-filling, are the death of education. They destroy the teachers' interest and initiative.

The human being is not an object to be manipulated and slotted into a system. He has a personal destiny. He is an evolving spiritual entity, a creation of the gods in a continual process of evolution.

To take part in a materialistic technical culture, learning is not enough. The self must be strong, not in the egoistical sense but in the way it can respond to negative influences. The human being cannot escape—indeed, should not seek to escape—worldly experiences, but he must be in a position to discriminate and not be dominated by them.

# 6. THE THREEFOLD NATURE OF THE HUMAN BEING. THE TEMPERAMENTS

In Chapter 4, Phases of Development, we considered the human being in a fourfold aspect, that of physical body, etheric, astral and ego. This is one way of looking at him, but there are also others. For instance, there is a threefold aspect.

Human beings are gifted with a life of soul, and in the soul are the forces of thinking, feeling and willing. These forces have a bodily basis, and the teacher wishing to understand the human being will give some thought to these connections.

Let us take observation of the physical body as a starting point.

The first thing that strikes us is a certain polarity—head and limbs, not a threefoldness but a duality. While there is the possibility of the head forming free-ranging, universal thoughts, the limbs are fettered to the earth. Symbolically we see heaven and earth, spirit and matter.

The head is round, hard without, soft within. It gives the impression of independence, being finely balanced on the vertebral column and carried around like a fine lady or gentleman, viewing the surroundings and receiving sense impressions through eyes, nose, ears and tongue without much effort. In the head is the brain, the organ of consciousness. The brain, with its cranial nerves and the spinal cord with the nerves which flow to it, constitutes the central nervous system. The brain is immersed in fluid and thus the downward pressure is almost eliminated. While the rest of the body is pulled down by gravity, this organ of consciousness is buoyant—a sign that our thinking can range far and wide.

If we look at the lower half of the human being and assume that for a moment we see only bones, then the pelvis, by comparison with the head, is an open construction in front of which are the organs of digestion and reproduction. The legs extend, radial-like. The hard bone is within, the soft flesh without. The legs carry the body, leaving the arms, their close relatives, free to create and manipulate.

However, there is a third constituent member, and this is the thorax, containing the heart and the lungs. In this area bone is interspersed with muscular tissue to allow flexibility in breathing. The upper bones are small and more tightly held, tending in form towards the head. The lower ones are more open, and the lowest of all, called floating ribs, are fixed only at one end. Thus they have more of the character of the limbs.

Together with the heart the lungs form the rhythmic system. From the moment of birth to the moment of death these systems are at work, day and night, without respite— unlike head and limbs, which take time off. The principle of breathing is the principle of life—inspiration, expiration. It is the yearly rhythm of the seasons, in night and day, sleeping and waking. It is the principle of plant growth.

The brain in the head is the bodily basis of thinking. Here the human being is most conscious. With the limbs, man performs deeds in the outer world. The brain may be conscious of the deed but the arm that wields the broom and the hand that holds it are not. Neither are we normally conscious of activities that take place in the abdomen. The limbs are the bodily basis of willing.

Periodically, the brain and limbs rest. This is not the case in the middle region, as already noted. Here is a region of semi-consciousness. We can be aware of our breathing and pulse beat—or not. A shock will cause the heart to stop beating for a moment. Embarrassment causes blushing. Exciting news causes a change in the breathing rate. Thus the rhythmic system can be considered the bodily basis of feeling.

As, however, the various parts of the body function independently and yet interdependently, so it is with the activities described above. In any one of these the others are present.

Although we can ascribe thinking to the head, feeling to the rhythmic system and willing to the limbs, these are only the physical instruments. The activities are not initiated in these regions.

The forces of thinking, feeling and willing lie, as stated, in the soul, which consists of astral substance. The astral body is the bearer of pleasure, pain, joy or sorrow, which are caused by outside stimuli. They contribute to form a sort of personalized entity of this substance. This provides one side of soul nature. Another comes from the fact that the soul also receives supersensible impressions—ideas and impulses which are of spiritual origin and lift the human being above the animal. In so far as the ego can command the soul it can transform it and develop new faculties.

Modern education tends to lay stress on intellectual activities and a balance is sought by physical exercise. The third force is overlooked and it is just this middle region that Steiner education seeks to cultivate. That is why an artistic approach is taken in the most formative years and why so much art is practised in the Waldorf school. Art has the effect of harmonizing these forces.

## The Temperaments

In the individual's life on this earth certain characteristics manifest themselves that are known as the temperaments. They are the result of events and experiences in a previous existence.

In the chapter on evolution, the fourfold development of

the earth is described—warmth, gaseous substances, liquid, solid. There is a parallel in our four elements of fire, air, water, earth. These four elements, in a transposed form, are also to be found in the human being. A preponderance of one or the other gives a person his temperament. This is to be looked at figuratively, although to some extent it is also apparent in the physical.

It is only intended to draw attention to these matters here. They are dealt with at length in most books on Steiner education.

The fire element manifests in the choleric. Choler comes from a Greek word meaning bile, a yellow liquid contained in the gall bladder to aid digestion. To have the 'gall' to do something means to have the impudence or the arrogance. The choleric person is the mover of mountains, bossy, convinced of his infallibility. He is an entrepreneur but cannot be bothered with detail. He is fixed in purpose and if not crossed can be kind and generous.

The sanguine is the airy one. Our general use of the word sanguine describes the character very well. The word itself means 'blood' and blood is something which is continually on the move. To be in movement is very typical of the sanguine person, be it in body or in mind. Such a person is lively, talkative and interested in everything but usually superficially so. He is full of ideas, likes change and is very sociable.

Phlegm originally meant inflammation, but the word was then applied to the sticky substance which gets stuck at the back of the throat. The phlegmatic is connected with the watery element. He has a stolid and undemonstrative disposition. He is easygoing and apparently a dreamer—but this should not be mistaken for what is really going on in his mind, for he is exercising judgement. He is reliable and conscientious.

Melancholy means black bile, a picture for one who finds life a burden or at least complains to the world that it is. A melancholic person is very much concerned with himself, introspective, with a feeling that everyone is his enemy. He is an intellectual and can be helpful if his sympathies are aroused.

All four temperaments exist in all of us but usually one predominates. They show themselves as inborn character-istics of the personality and have definite negative and positive aspects. If the individual possesses and can recognize negative traits, it is within his freedom to seek to overcome them.

The above notes, of course, apply to adults. In the case of children one has to be very careful in making judgements. One could say, for instance, that all children are sanguine; this is a characteristic of childhood. But children are easily affected by other factors, e.g. stomach troubles might result in outbursts of temper, or malfunction of an organ might make the child appear withdrawn. In such cases it could be wrong to deduce a choleric or a melancholic temperament respectively.

Observation of the child—its physical appearance, gait, eye movements, gestures, habits, attitudes, paintings and drawings—will provide clues.

These matters are detailed in the author's booklet *The Temperaments in Education*, where it is also explained how a knowledge of the temperaments is important in dealing with the various types of children.

# 7. CURRICULUM SUBJECTS: THE SPIRITUAL BACKGROUND

No attempt is made in the Waldorf school to teach spiritual science (Anthroposophy), or to indoctrinate the children in any way. The background knowledge is for teachers, and they will present their material objectively in the knowledge that what is considered scientific fact at one time is not necessarily scientific fact at another. They will, therefore, leave a space, through which other points of view will eventually appear.

Spiritual science agrees with the statement in the Bible that in the beginning God created the heaven and the earth. It may give a more detailed explanation but it accepts as fact that the world and man are divinely created, that the physical is a manifestation of the spirit and that spirit is to be found in the physical. This has a bearing naturally on what and how things are taught. For instance, the spiritual-scientific explanation of evolution is somewhat at variance with that generally accepted elsewhere. However, the teaching in the schools is not dogmatic and much depends on the teacher's skill in presentation. The ideas can only be put forward along with others, and the Darwinistic and Laplace theories have also to be accommodated and explained. (An outline of the anthroposophical view on evolution will be found later in this book.)

If the world is of divine creation, then obviously all within it has a spiritual origin. The Bible statement may be interpreted in various ways but it indisputedly contains the idea of spiritual origins. Whether one believes this or not is another matter but spiritual science accepts it as basic truth and extends the concept of God to include ranks of spiritual beings (see Chapter 9, Unseen Forces). It is the weaving and interweaving of these beings that results in the creation of the material world and its contents. It is thus the basis of all sciences that have to do with substance.

Similarly, mathematics is based on the activity of spiritual beings whose manifestations are revealed in the harmony of number, rhythms and form. This is not a new idea. The Chaldeans—great mathematicians and astronomers—saw the manifestation of the gods in the movement of the heavenly bodies. Plato, the Greek philosopher, demanded of his pupils that they must have schooling in geometry or mathematics. He is reported as saying, 'God geometrizes,' meaning, according to Rudolf Steiner, that God creates with such inner force as is used in mathematical thinking. We have already mentioned Kepler who considered the laws of planetary movement to be an expression of divine creative powers.

Music and language have their origins in the 'Music of the Spheres', a phrase sometimes looked upon as a poetic fantasy but one which actually has a real spiritual content.

Every schoolboy and every schoolgirl has to learn the theorem of Pythagoras, but Pythagoras was much more than a mathematician. He was a philosopher and the founder of an esoteric school which greatly influenced the development of mathematics and its application to music and astronomy. He speaks also of this 'Music of the Spheres'.

Another great historical figure, Shakespeare, also refers to the phenomenon. In *The Merchant of Venice*, Lorenzo speaks of the floor of heaven inlaid with patines (metal plates) of bright gold:

There's not the smallest orb that thou behold'st
But in his motion like an angel sings,
Still quiring to the young-eyed cherubins;
Such harmony is in immortal souls:
But, whilst this muddy vesture of decay
Doth grossly close it in, we cannot hear it.

What is this 'Music of the Spheres'? It is a supersensible experience of the initiate who can penetrate to higher realms and can hear—so to speak—the voices of the gods. Those who have such a gift tell us that music and language are reflections of these heavenly voices.

With regard to history, art and religion, it is possible to be much more specific about the spiritual background.

## History

Since history comprises all that has happened from the beginning of time to the present, it is no wonder that the mind boggles at the thought of trying to digest it and represent it to children at school.

It is obvious that the study of history will yield an immense stream of fascinating and interesting facts, but to understand history the facts and events must be seen as revelations of forces which may not be immediately perceptible.

The following is taken from the preface of the author's book *Teaching History*, Vol. 1:

> History is the story of the development of mankind, but as humanity is made up of individuals history is also the story of man. The human being himself goes through an evolution and here we are not thinking in the Darwinian sense, but in the sense of the development of the mind. The modern human mind works in a certain way. In ancient times it was different. It is this change in the state of the mind which brings about the external changes, i.e. the scenes or phenomena of history. History is not merely a sequence of events. The sequences are dependent on the evolution of the mind. That is to say, history is not something which takes place only on the physical plane. The events are the manifestations of spiritual impulses

which arise within the human soul. It is feasible to think of such impulses being given by superhuman agencies. One has only to think of the inspiration given to the founders of the great religions, to the prophets of the Old Testament, or to consider the voices heard by Joan of Arc. That there can be negative influences is also fairly obvious. We have experienced madmen like Caligula. In more recent times one might even think of a Hitler being influenced or possessed by demonic beings.

What is this change which has taken place? We can look upon the evolution of man as a development of individuality, as a development of ego-consciousness, and along with this there goes a deeper penetration into the physical world. We can see a parallel to this in the growth of the individual human being.

The small child lives in a dreamlike state and is directed by the more mature adults. In the course of time he becomes independent, conscious of himself as an individual, aware of his own ego, and he learns to cope with the material world. In earlier civilizations the mass of the people lived in a childlike state and were guided and directed by personalities who in some respects were more mature, i.e. their priests and kings. These, in turn, were guided by spiritual beings (gods) and were what are known as 'initiates', by which is meant that they had direct experience of a supersensible world. The development has been from this state of dreamlike dependence to the self-reliant, self-consciousness of today.

The change, of course, does not reveal itself uniformly over the whole world. When we speak of the development of mankind or the evolution of man in this sense, we refer to the fresh impulse which manifests itself in the peak civilization of the time. Thus, for instance, while something new was appearing in Greece, there were other cultures in existence (China, India) and what we term primitive peoples which were remnants from the past.

To illustrate this development the Waldorf history curriculum brings, at about the age of 11, stories and descriptions of the series of civilizations that portray this thread. Before these are given, however, children have received what might be termed a preface.

In Class 3, at the age of 9, stories from the Old Testament are told as stories, and included of course is the biblical account of creation. This presents in picture form what is described later in this book as the planetary evolution (see Appendix).

The Old Testament leads from prehistoric to historic times, from a description of a divine creation to trials and tribulations in the physical world and the advent of a Saviour. The mighty pictures given show the progress of human development. Humanity, created in spiritual heights, enters the material world and strives towards independence. The stories present an objective picture of man's development and thus strengthen, albeit unconsciously, the inner growth of the child. (These matters are dealt with at length in the author's book *Commentary on the Old Testament Stories*.)

At the age of 11 children begin to develop a sense for what is historical, and this is then the right time to present pictures of the civilizations mentioned which stretch from Atlantis* to the present. Without it being actually said in so

* According to legend, Atlantis was a continent where the waters of the Atlantic ocean now roll. Spiritual science confirms the existence of this continent and equates the story of Noah and the flood with its disappearance. Noah, also known as Manu, was one of the great initiates of the time who was aware of things to come and led a group of people to a safe area in central Asia where the earth was more consolidated. From here initiatives radiated to form new civilizations.

Atlantis, of course, did not disappear after 40 days and nights of rain. The '40' signifies a very long period, but the end of the continent is dated about 8000 BC

Groups of peoples had settled all over the globe and developed according to their dispositions and environments.

many words, these descriptions also contain the idea of the spiritual development of man from the time of direct contact with, and dependence on, the Divinity to a time of independence and self-consciousness. As a further educational factor they also mirror the individual development from babyhood to self-conscious maturity—in other words, the full incarnation of the ego.

In the Upper School these matters become subjects for discussion in the context of philosophy, history, religion or wherever they are appropriate. In no circumstances is an effort made to indoctrinate, but the idea of evolution towards something greater is made clear and this gives students a positive outlook and a hold in life.

From about the age of 11 then, a picture of the progressive civilizations is presented. To learn about the early ones, i.e. Ancient India and Iran, we must rely on myths and the results of spiritual investigation; for the later ones we have historical records.

Each cultural epoch of post-Atlantis lasts approximately 2000 years. Let us consider this aspect.

Our present age dates from the Renaissance, 1313. Rome was founded about 740 BC. The Egypto-Chaldean epoch began about 3000 BC—in each case a period of about 2000 years. Iranian culture would thus be dated about 5000 BC, and Ancient India somewhat earlier than 7000 BC.

The Holy Rishis or Sages were leaders in the first of these cultures, centred in present-day India. The myths that have come down to us give a flavour of attitudes at the time. The earth was not quite real, people's souls longed for their home in the heavenly regions; they had direct contact with the spirit.

The scene shifts to Iran and Iranian culture, led by the great initiate, Zarathustra. The minds of people were turned towards the earth. Agriculture became a holy duty. It was realized that life was a continual struggle between the forces of darkness and those of light, between Ahriman and Ahura-Mazda.

The next civilization was that of Egypt/Chaldea. In Egypt the Pharaoh was priest and king. His path to the spirit had to be attained by long and arduous preparation. Society was organized under his direction and that of his priests. Bodies were mummified. There was growing interest in death and the beyond. A form of writing was created. Craftsmen, doctors, mathematicians, astronomers, even bankers flourished!

The consciousness of the spirit world was receding. The physical was becoming of more importance. The enormous temples are witness to a desire to experience a greatness which was now eluding the people. The Chaldeans studied the stars as a manifestation of the divine.

Very noticeable new impulses manifest themselves in the Graeco-Roman period. The gods, of which there are many, assume an almost human characteristic. Philosophy and the power of thinking were born. These take the place of direct spiritual vision. The new-found power of thought is directed to the physical world. Individualities make their mark. Worldly empires are built. Law as between man and man is established. A man, the emperor, is elevated to the position of a god. Into the Roman world Christ was born, a theme which will be touched upon later. Rome degenerated and with it the Roman world outwardly disintegrated, but it left a distinct influence in Europe.

A new impulse was born in the fifteenth century and what then made its appearance is still with us in increasing strength. Its centre was Europe. Europeans sought truth through natural science. God was relegated to second place or even discarded. Their probings brought about immense discoveries in all fields of knowledge. European influence spread around the world and fathered the present materialistic culture.

Through these successive civilizations we can trace a change of consciousness. In the older cultures men had a certain clairvoyant vision and no feeling of personality. In the course of development, spiritual vision gives place to thinking; and the feeling of belonging to a group gives way to the feeling of ego-consciousness.

It would seem from the present state of modern society that mankind has arrived at a crossroads. Culture centred on purely natural-scientific attitudes has not produced the promised paradise. In fact the path seems to go downhill. There is, however, a change in thinking in the modern world, and ideas and movements are developing based on a realization that there are factors in life beyond the economic and political.

Since evolution is a continuing process we must assume that it will continue, but there are two directions. One leads to degeneration and increasing chaos. The other will establish a new and, it is to be hoped, a better order. A prerequisite for the latter is the recognition of the spiritual world and the understanding of the path mankind has travelled so far.

The human being was created by God and endowed with godlike qualities. He has been divinely guided, but in the course of evolution he has achieved a certain independence from the gods with the possibility of furthering, or otherwise, his own development. Through contact with the material world he has achieved ego-consciousness. With this consciousness and with the powers bestowed on him by higher powers, he can now transform himself, developing by himself those faculties by which he becomes aware of the spiritual world. In contrast to his earlier experience he will now be conscious of both matter and spirit. His knowledge will be whole, and from spiritual knowledge will flow initiative and inspiration.

In the cycle of cultural epochs we can anticipate further civilizations and even transformations of the earth.

## Art

Art has many facets, many interpretations and gives rise to many opinions. It has a particular place in the Waldorf school since it is accepted here that art arises as an expression of the spiritual/supersensible in physical form.

As far as Waldorf education is concerned, art could be considered under three headings:

1 Its use as a means of education
2 As an illustration of the development of mankind
3 Its intrinsic educational value

1. It has already been explained that, particularly in the years from 7 to 14, an artistic approach to teaching is demanded by the nature of the child. This means teaching in an imaginative, pictorial manner and not in intellectual concepts.

Drawing, painting and modelling are all used in furthering the work, but this could perhaps be termed illustrating rather than aiming at the production of masterpieces—although many of the results could claim to have artistic merit. Such activity affords great satisfaction to the soul.

These pursuits are not one-sided as is a purely academic subject or a physical exercise but they occupy heart, mind and will and thus engage all faculties of thinking, feeling and willing and bring them into a certain state of balance.

2. Looking back into the past we can see that art arose as spiritual vision began to fade. When man was in direct contact with the gods he had no need for art, but when the gods withdrew (that is, when he lost the vision) he felt the need for some tangible expression of spirituality. One result of this was religious observance, but art also arose out of religion. We have stated that in the course of evolution the mind of man changes, but with it so does his art. A glance at history illustrates the point.

No one who has visited Egypt and seen the relics of its former civilization can fail to be impressed by its works of art—its paintings, drawings, sculptures and buildings. Perhaps the most impressive, at least for enormity of size, are the pyramids, closely followed by the temple at Karnak and the reconstructed edifice lifted out of the reach of Lake Nasser at Abu Simbel.

The pyramids are huge constructions of blocks of masonry, built on a square base with four triangular sides meeting in a point. The four sides face the four cardinal points. The square is a symbol of the earth and the triangle that of the Divinity.

They are not temples and it has been assumed that they were the burial places of the Pharaohs but no corpse has ever been found in any of them. The clue to their use may lie in an early Egyptian text which, concerning the pyramid, states: 'A staircase to heaven is laid for Pharaoh that he may ascend to heaven thereby.' This could of course be taken as a path to the spiritual world after death but it could also mean that it was a place from which the soul of the Pharaoh was projected into the spiritual world, i.e. the pyramid was a place of initiation.

Egyptian temples were also massive structures which certainly give the impression of earthly weight. The rooms in them get smaller and smaller as one approaches the altar. Can we explain these facts?

We have already referred to human development both in the history of civilizations and in the growth of the individual human being as a descent from the spirit into matter.

One explanation of the huge Egyptian constructions could be that the direct experience of the divine-spiritual world was fading and that it was being replaced by massive edifices expressing the power of the Godhead in physical form. The fact of the progressive smallness of rooms could be symbolic of man incarnating.

If we look at Egyptian sculptures of human beings, one thing is very noticeable and that is the blank look in their facial expression. They seem to be staring into space. Perhaps the emptiness suggests that the mind is absent but is tuned in to heavenly voices.

Another great figure in Egyptian sculpture is the Sphinx, which is a huge stone carving with a human head and a lion's body. It expresses the duality of the human being— enlightenment in the head, animal passions in the body.

In the graphic arts are depicted connections with the divine. The name of the script, hieroglyphics, means 'sacred writing'. The absence of certain colours in the paintings would point to a different experience in sense-perception.

By contrast with the Egyptian temples let us consider those of Greece. Whoever has also stood in the ruins of the temple of Poseidon on Cape Sounio will appreciate the enormous difference. Here on the hill is light and space, evoking a feeling very different from the depressing solidity of Egypt. Here one can feel an expression of balance, of light and dark, an expression of harmony between the forces of earth and those of heaven.

Contrasting Greek statues of the human being with those of Egypt, we note that the former have an element of dynamism and individual expression.

In the field of painting the Greek experience of colour also seems to have been different from our own, which would point to a different mentality.

The great change in consciousness that took place in Greek times is that people began to have a greater feeling for themselves as individuals. That led them to ponder on their relationships with the rest of the world and this led to the birth of philosophy. The consideration of their relationship to the gods resulted in Drama.

Moving westwards in Europe, to the setting for the next great epoch of civilization, we see a different state of mind finding expression in the beautiful Gothic cathedrals, with their spires and pointed arches, demonstrating the desire of the soul to strive upwards towards God.

These magnificent buildings, however, mark a culmination of Christian art which really begins with mosaics and paintings of biblical scenes. The earliest painters used a golden background which gives the pictures an atmosphere of holiness, in reality a reflection of the spiritual world. Gradually, paintings came to have a more earthly aspect. Perspective was introduced and a background of trees and hills. An individual quality comes to expression in human faces.

In the Renaissance, personalities and human emotions are portrayed. In the work of the great artists we see expressions of piety, wisdom and love in the human soul, combined with artistic striving to reproduce nature but not merely to copy it.

As people became more interested in material things, landscape painting and realistic pictures began to appear. The scene moves to everyday things. As the feeling for individuality develops so does portrait painting.

The above historical survey is a very shortened version of what is studied in Class 9 in the Waldorf school under the heading History of Art. It illustrates the theme of the changing mind of man from an awareness of the spiritual world to a consciousness of the physical and the accompanying feeling of individuality.

The same theme is to be found in the history of poetry, literature and music.

3. We see then that the origins of art lie in the religious life. But what is the present position? What of art in the school?

The supersensible origin of art has been forgotten. Nevertheless the desire for artistic expression is still deeply seated in the human soul. For instance, we may contemplate a beautiful landscape, but unless we have become totally indifferent through being immersed in materialism there is always a feeling of something we do not quite grasp. Secrets are hidden in nature, and an artist feels the urge to probe them and express them, adding something or, so to speak, going beyond nature. He has a need to satisfy unconscious impulses.

The mere reproduction of the world, exactly as it is, can never be art in the real sense. There would be no point in it. No copy of nature will be as good as nature herself. In painting, for instance, exact reproduction would not allow for any imaginative or emotional content. Art requires a spark of visionary insight. In painting an artist has to grasp the essence, maybe mood, in a landscape and interpret it in colour. Painting a portrait does not mean producing only a lifelike picture, but it seeks to show the spirit of the person shining through the form and the colour. It is as if the artist expresses something in the perceptible that has been hidden.

In a sculpture something must be incorporated that is not mere copy. The Greeks had this ability.

In poetry the combination of sound, rhyme and rhythm lifts speech into another world. Music is a manifestation of a spiritual experience.

There is an artist in every one of us. Artistic appreciation belongs to the totality of life. Within us is the urge to grasp the world aesthetically. This can be understood if we merely consider what is termed 'taste', although the experience may be subconscious. Certain colours harmonize with one another, others clash. Hence the sense of 'dress' and the desire for harmonious furnishings in the home.

Today, however, there seems to be a trend in sections of our modern society which prefers what is vulgar and unaesthetic—psychedelic colour schemes, caterwauling that passes for singing, cacophonic noise instead of music and concrete blocks for buildings. These are symptoms of a loss of sense for what is beautiful.

An education, such as is given in the Waldorf school,

offers the opportunity of developing an aesthetic sensibility and artistic appreciation in painting, sculpting, music, poetry, together of course with learning the necessary skills and disciplines. In the practice of all these arts there is an element of the unseen, the spiritual.

The impulse to the practice of art comes from the spiritual world. Artistic imagination is a step towards that world. In a work of art something related to supersensible knowledge appears.

## *Religion*

Waldorf education was founded in Christian Europe and its main spread has been in countries which, at least nominally, accept Christianity. Although the Waldorf schools have a Christian background, it is not the task of the teacher to make children adherents of the Christian faith. In the religion lessons of the Waldorf school there is nothing doctrinal or dogmatic and certainly no hint of sectarianism.

(In view of the fact that Waldorf education has now found a footing in countries with different traditions— Japan, India, Egypt, Israel, Africa—and also the fact that ethnic mixtures are now found in schools, some rethinking of certain aspects of presentation may be necessary, a matter not discussed here.)

According to its derivation the word religion means a 'binding together' or a 're-uniting'. It expresses the belief in the connection of divine powers with human destiny. It is therefore obvious that an education based on spiritual science will be a religious one.

This does not mean that the teacher is forever preaching or sermonizing; neither does he come into the classroom with the announcement that he is about to describe the work of the Hierarchies in creation, or life after death, or any such esoteric matter.

It must be repeated that these things are background study for the teacher's understanding and definitely not a part of the curriculum.

Religious education is a general term which means learning to appreciate that the material world is not the be-all and end-all of existence but that there is a spiritual dimension. This is a fundamental attitude throughout the school which permeates all subjects. Let us first consider its general application and then the specific religion lessons.

Naturally, all teaching has to be based on the age of the children concerned. The material and the way it is presented will change accordingly.

Small children feel an affinity with the entire world—the winds, the trees, the birds, the animals, with fellow humans. One could say that they have a *natural* religion. Before the age of 9 no child has difficulty with the concept of God or angels or fairies. Fairy-tales, legends, Old Testament stories (at 9) provide ample evidence of the immanence of unseen or divine powers. Children at this age are innocent and feel that the world is good. The fairy-tales provide evidence of how the good overcomes evil. They are archetypes of human destiny. They have a profound importance for the whole of life. This is not only through the content of the stories but through the fact that they stimulate creative imagination which leads to cognitive powers and social abilities.

At the age of 9 and 10 children come down a little further into the material world, and in the normal course of teaching they are given a Practical Activities period, usually farming, gardening, and house-building.

Besides describing these activities and, where feasible, getting the children to participate in them, it is possible to cultivate a religious attitude. This is not done by precepts; the process is a little more subtle. Awe, reverence, wonder and gratitude are all feelings allied to those of religion and they can be awakened objectively if the following train of thought is followed.

The farmer is the guardian (not the exploiter) of the soil and responsible for its products. But he has to work with Mother Nature (God) who provides the earth in the first place, and also the plants, the rain and the sunshine. That a tiny seed produces an ear of corn, or an acorn a mighty oak tree, or an animal produces its young, is a mighty achievement, the realization of which will excite a feeling of wonder. And let us not forget that wonder is the source of all wisdom.

The subject of house-building can open paths to many considerations. First there is the comparison of the house with our body. We live in a house as the spirit lives in our body. We even go in and out. Then there is the idea of shelter, of using what nature gives to construct a place to cut oneself off from her. The third is the question of materials. Who provides them? Earth? God? And fourth is the realization that so many skills are needed and not only the skills of those actually working but of those who provide and transport the timber, the bricks, the various fittings and materials. There is a long chain which not only arouses wonder but should stimulate a social understanding.

In the subsequent classes one has to deal with the sciences such as chemistry and physics, and it may be thought that no great religious feelings can be attached to these. Again, it is a matter of attitude on the part of the teacher. Chemical and physical processes, whether they are natural or contrived, can call forth feelings of great wonder and astonishment. In the former case one can think of volcanoes, northern lights, phosphorescence, sea and air currents, the rain cycle; in the latter, laboratory experiments, industrial processes, the general application in practical life. Of the greatest wonder perhaps is the mind of man, which can encompass all these things.

All teaching will be more acceptable if the human element is taken into account. There is warmth in the blood, warmth in the soul, light in the eyes, air and liquid coursing through the body.

When things are considered in their relationship to the human being, the human being feels himself also as part of the world, a world in which unseen forces also play a part.

Other themes might be on colour and the rainbow, the action of acids, the formation of common salt (sodium chloride) and—a particular eye-opener—the demonstration that water is a compound of two gases, hydrogen and oxygen ($H_2O$).

In the Upper School, plant growth and plant life, the study of animals and man—botany, zoology, anthropology, anatomy, physiology—all provide substance for the development of religious feelings.

A useful study could be made of the comparison between stone, plant, animal and man.

The above describes the general attitude towards religion in the Waldorf school. We will now refer to the actual lessons, which are usually given twice a week.

The prime purpose of the religion lesson is to cultivate a special feeling or attitude, something akin to what is produced at a religious service. Anyone who has told young children a fairy-story will have observed the sigh of satisfaction with which it has been received. The soul has been nourished, and this is the basic aim of the religion lesson.

It is usual to open such lessons with a prayer or a verse, and a special one was given by Rudolf Steiner for this purpose, affirming the presence of the spirit (God) both in nature and in the human being, and unity.

From Class 5 upwards the Lord's Prayer would be an alternative, but since it is often gabbled without much thought, attention should be called to its contents so that it is spoken with understanding.

First there is an affirmation of the divine foundation of the world; then an appeal for spiritual and physical integration. There follows a request that our physical needs may be met, that we may make compensation for our mistakes, that we may not give way to unworthy impulses and not sink into the evil of materialism.

Inspiration for the lessons can be drawn from any source. One could think of the words of the Duke in Shakespeare's *As You Like It* (Act 2, Scene 1): 'Our life ... finds tongues in trees, books in the running brooks, sermons in stones and good in everything.' One might suspect that the words good and God are related, and if we say 'God in everything' then we have an expression for the religious element in education.

To meet the soul requirements of the different ages, three groupings are necessary: 6 to 9, 10 to 14, 15 to 18.

For the young children, fairy-stories are useful as they stand, particularly those of the brothers Grimm, but the teacher should use original texts and not doctored copies. A special selection might be made for the religion lesson which would include those with a cosmic dimension, such as Mother Holle, Hansel and Gretel, Cinderella (see the author's book *The Interpretation of Fairy Tales*).

Stories of elemental beings and angels can be told and the facts of sleeping and waking revealed in story form, i.e. in sleep a visit is made to another kingdom to meet the angels. Old Testament stories are suitable for children aged 9 to 10. They may have been dealt with in the Main Lesson period but, even if they have, there is no harm in repetition.

Between the ages of 9 and 12, stories of heroes and reformers are appropriate. They illustrate the unconquerable human spirit. At 11 to 12, stories from Shakespeare can be used; also the stories of King Arthur and his knights. Now is the time to introduce the New Testament and learn about the life of Christ.

In a course on religion (available only to teachers of religion in Waldorf schools) Dr Hahn, the course leader, makes the following suggestions for this age group:

1. Take the sun as a theme. Consider how it accompanies us throughout the year but has different appearances— spring, summer, autumn, winter. It sends warmth and light with observable results on plants, animals and humans. The power given by the sun in spring and summer results in the harvest of autumn. We collect the fruits of the earth and consume stored sunshine in the winter. As we harvest the green of the leaves turns to colours; the days become shorter. With the darkness comes All Soul's Day when we remember the dead who have entered another world. Four weeks before Christmas is the time of Advent, a time when we begin to look forward to the Christmas festival when the one whose birthday we celebrate was called the Light of the World.

2. Make a study of the rose, note its scent and form, the beautiful flower and the unpleasant thorns. Ancient Persians were the first cultivators of the rose. To them it was a symbol of the struggle between the light and the dark. Most flowers have national or local names, but the rose is a rose, with slight variations in spelling, in all European languages. It was spread by the Romans whose material civilization engulfed Europe. Now it is a symbol of love.

3. Compare it with the lily and the lily's overpowering scent. The lily is associated with death and burials.

Read Charles Dickens's *Christmas Carol*, recommended by Dr Steiner as it shows how something like a Christmas present comes to expression through wise helping powers.

In the next age group, 15 to 18, the power of the individuality begins to assert itself. Material for religion lessons is to be found in biographies, particularly those where a turning-point occurs in life through unforeseen circumstances. Wrestling with fate, as portrayed in the story of Helen Keller, is also a wonderful theme. (Helen Keller,

1880–1986, born blind, deaf and mute, learned to read, write and speak, became an author and achieved academic distinction.)

Other suitable stories include those of Parzival, the Templars and the Buddha. The Acts of the Apostles and certain of St Paul's epistles provide excellent material, e.g. 1 Corinthians, 13, which ends: And now abideth faith, hope and love, these three: but the greatest of these is love.

The above suggestions are more or less the ideal, but in present circumstances it is necessary to go beyond formal lessons to deal with present-day problems and open up a field for discussion.

For the higher age group (15 to 18), it is very important to discuss religion in connection with practical problems, especially those concerned with the existence of evil in the world today. Manifestations are abundant—rape, violence, drugs, wars, etc. The question is how inner religious and moral convictions can face up to such evils.

Although it is not standard practice, some schools invite adherents of all kinds of religious persuasions to address their twelfth class and explain their faiths and what they mean to them. Thus the pupils may hear from an Anglican, a Roman Catholic, an Evangelical, a Quaker, Buddhist, native African, Moslem, even a Scientologist. It is what 18-year-olds need and it gives them the opportunity of putting questions. At that age they wish to consider all options, and in the course of time they will decide on their own individual path.

**Note:** When the first Waldorf school opened in Stuttgart, it was the custom for the ministers or priests of the various denominations to come into the school to give religion lessons to their respective flocks. These were considered extra-curricular, and children attended at the wish of their parents. At the time there was no problem with non-Christian minorities.

Since a great number of children had no particular allegiance, the so-called independent religion lesson was introduced, but also as an ex-curricular activity.

The habit of receiving visiting clergy into the school has fallen into disuse and now it is usual for two religion lessons weekly to be incorporated into the curriculum.

Non-committed parents of the original Waldorf school had expressed the wish for children to receive a deeper religious experience, and so the question of a non-denominational service was discussed and eventually organized. This arrangement has been adopted by many other schools, and now Sunday services, taken by teachers especially appointed for the task, are organized for those children whose parents wish them to attend.

These are special occasions, separate from the normal religion lessons in class outlined above.

# 8. DESTINY AND KARMA: EDUCATION FOR ETERNITY

An epitaph, written by Benjamin Franklin for himself at the age of 23, provides a good introduction to this subject.

The Body
of
Benjamin Franklin
Printer
Like the cover of an old book,
Its contents worn out
And stripped of its lettering and gilding,
Lies here, food for worms.
But the work shall not be lost,
For it will, as he believed, appear once more,
In a new and more elegant edition,
Revised and corrected
by
The Author

Steiner education is concerned with all-round development, which includes body, soul and spirit—and thus a knowledge of matters beyond what is merely physical is an obvious requirement.

The idea was already indicated in Chapter 7 that what we bring with us at birth in the way of abilities or talents (or the lack of them) can be considered as the result of our actions in the last life or earlier ones. We also come with certain desires or impulses inherited from previous existences.

We could also express this idea another way and say that we bring with us our destiny or karma. These words, however, may require a little clarification.

In thinking of destiny we usually have in mind the idea of a predetermined course of events or possibly the power which determines it. Karma expresses a related idea but has a somewhat different significance.

Karma is a word borrowed from Sanskrit and has the meaning of 'action' or 'effect'. The law of karma is one of cause and effect applied to our deeds. Used in the spiritual-scientific sense, it means that whatever is done in one life has an effect on the next. Rudolf Steiner expresses it thus: 'Activity that has become destiny is karma ... The spirit that reincarnates finds within the physical world the result of its deeds as destiny.' (*Reincarnation and Karma.*)

St Paul, in his letter to the Galatians, expressed the idea in a few succinct words: 'Whatsoever a man soweth, that shall he also reap.'

One way of understanding how karma works is to think of our daily life. If we indulge in an excess of food and drink, we are sick. That is not karma but foolishness, but it illustrates the law of cause and effect in simple terms.

A further help to understanding is to consider the rhythm of day and night, waking and sleeping and the extension of the idea to birth and death.

During the day we are awake and active; at night we sleep and our consciousness is blotted out. However, when we wake in the morning we may feel with Goethe's Faust that 'Life's pulses now with fresher force awaken' but we do not start our lives afresh. Similarly, when we die we relinquish a physical body for a while, during which time we refresh ourselves—restore or rebuild ourselves might be better expressions—and then return to inhabit our new body. Since the world has changed during our absence, we have to spend some time getting used to it and this is our childhood.

A significant point may be understood concerning destiny by comparing human growth with that of an animal, even those nearest to us. After the animal is born it matures quickly in great contrast to the human being who needs time to grow because he is destined for further development.

Just as the activities of one day are carried over to the next and possibly beyond, so it is with our activities in succeeding incarnations. We may have been engaged with a certain task one day and the next we finish it or continue to work at it. Yesterday, or the day or week before, we had dealings with certain people; tomorrow or next week we shall meet them again. One day we learn to do something, we practise and soon we have acquired a skill. A simple example is learning to read. At school we learn the alphabet and the way letters are put together to form words, but do we remember the process of learning? In most cases the answer is no, but we now have the ability to read and even to understand what we read.

A similar process takes place from one incarnation to the next.

Of a genius we say: He/She is gifted. We are all gifted in some measure. But the origin of 'gifts' is effort. We learn something in one incarnation and acquire a skill. This is transformed and becomes a talent. One example cited is how a study of harmonies and rhythms in music could lead to a gift for mathematics.

The idea of reaping as one sows also extends to the differing circumstances in people's lives. It is obvious that these are not equal. Some people are rich, some are poor. Some seem to have an easy path, some a difficult one. This also applies to matters of health.

Whatever the circumstances may be, it must be realized that as human beings we have ourselves chosen them in order to further our development. Poor circumstances and difficult situations generally mean that we have put ourselves in a position to develop strengths in which we were lacking. This should not be interpreted dogmatically since outside influences such as wars, earthquakes, etc., can change the course of events. Good conditions provide us with the opportunity, or indeed put the obligation upon us, to further the general good as well as ourselves.

If one can accept the idea of karma, then it is not so difficult to understand that also the effect of one's attitudes in one incarnation will manifest in another. Positive attitudes produce positive results and vice versa. Rudolf Steiner gives specific instances of these. For instance, those who speak and love the truth will experience joy, inner satisfaction and possess intelligence. Those who take no interest in spiritual matters will be dull in the next life.

It must not be thought that karma is blind fate or the will of Allah. Karma teaches that we have willed what happens to us. We have brought it with us from previous existences and it is incorporated in our being. We experience it as desires, impulses, urges or deeds which we carry out through sympathy or antipathy although we are not conscious of the karmic connection. Subconsciously we are led to certain situations or to meet certain people but karma does not dictate how to proceed.

It provides opportunities and situations. What we do with them is for us to decide when we meet them. Our present conscious actions are not decided by fate.

The study of karma is an important chapter of spiritual science and an important chapter for the teacher.

We have already explained that education requires the very widest possible curriculum. Education is not a matter of handing out so much information which can be regurgitated at will, but of helping the individuality to find its right place in life. For this purpose not only the necessary skills must be taught but the mind opened out to all possibilities.

In a previous chapter, child growth and development were described in terms of soul-spirit incarnating into a physical body. Unless the teacher is an initiate, which is unlikely, he does not know the spiritual background of the pupils in front of him, whether they are potential Einsteins or Shakespeares. If the thought does not cause him direct anxiety, it may at least lead him to consider his own position and may make him less inclined to pontificate. Teachers do not know immediately what hidden talents or impulses exist in the children before them and this is one of the reasons why every subject must be taught, or at least introduced, so that whatever faculty is slumbering be awakened.

A further point with regard to karma could be mentioned here. Children come into a certain school and a certain class and they are surrounded by a group of their peers. They are taught by certain teachers. One might ask if there is any special connection between teachers and those who are taught. Certainly the teacher may notice that some children have a particular relationship with one another, maybe friendly, maybe otherwise. It would be wrong to jump to conclusions but he might consider it a possibility that these relationships derive from the past.

The implications for the teacher are obvious. In the case of personal difficulties among the children he might have a role in finding a solution. It is within his power not only to develop the children's interests but also their moral and social attitudes.

In the light of reincarnation, teachers have an almost overwhelmingly responsible task. They are influencing the child, or rather the individuality, not only for present existence but for eternity.

So far in this chapter we have considered the effect of one life on the next and pointed to the role of education in this respect. But also to be considered is the life between incarnations, when the human being lives in the spiritual world. There his experiences continue and these are directly related to his past life. Education therefore has its after-effects in the life between death and rebirth, and what was stated earlier concerning learning and moral education is equally valid in this state of existence.

Death is an unavoidable, common experience, and conveys the idea of a certain finality. However, a great deal can be learnt about it by the study of spiritual-scientific literature. Since there is a general belief in some sort of life after death, it might be more appropriate to speak of the gateway of death; for death in this world means life in the beyond, in the spiritual world. Indeed the adepts tell us that it is a wonderful experience and that we pass on into a halo of light.

The departure from this world is the beginning of a great adventure. Rudolf Steiner gave a great many lectures on the subject, illustrating it from various points of view, and he also wrote about it in some of his books. Since his audiences and readers represented various cross-sections of humanity, he spoke or wrote in different ways and used a variety of terminology. In his explanations of events in the spiritual world he sometimes refers to human beings, the ego, the soul, the soul-spirit, and to regions, spheres or states of consciousness. (A summary of what he had to say on the subject is contained in the author's book *Rudolf Steiner — Aspects of his Spiritual World View*, Vol. 3, under the heading 'Life between Death and Rebirth'.)

Here we are concerned only with the subject in relation to education, and in order to make the account straightforward the descriptions following will be recorded as our own personal experiences using the collective pronoun 'we'.

At death we do not cease to exist. We cast off our physical body and enter the spiritual world, taking with us the fruits of our life on earth which will 'ripen' and be transformed for the next incarnation. Our experiences in this world are very much dependent on the sort of life we have led on earth. The old concept of hell for the wicked and heaven for the righteous may not be quite acceptable to modern thinking but it expresses a basic principle.

If we have lived irresponsible, dissolute lives, or if we

have become too engrossed in the pleasures of the flesh, we shall find ourselves in less comfortable circumstances for a while than our fellow humans who have been more conscientious and have been more devoted to ideals. Our contacts with others will depend on whether our interests on earth have been materialistic or spiritual; whether our attitudes have been altruistic or otherwise; whether we have been co-operative or the opposite, narrow or openminded, able to develop love and appreciation for all humanity, and to respect all religions.

It is, however, not only our relationships with our fellow human beings that are of consequence in the spiritual world but also our relationship with the higher beings who inhabit it.

Reference was already made to the concept of oneness, the idea of looking at the physical as a manifestation of the spiritual or the spiritual as the other side of the physical.

On earth we use our senses and live among the manifestations of the Divinity, among the deeds of the gods, or in a God-created world if the expression is preferred. In the spiritual world we live among the beings themselves, the creative forces.

When we pass into this world we meet these beings who rejoice, or otherwise, at what we bring with us. Their wellbeing is connected with our deeds and their task is to help us through this stage of our existence. They can bestow gifts in the measure in which we have earned them. The life we have lived on earth is therefore of great consequence.

As in the case of reincarnation and karma, the implications for education are clear.

# 9. UNSEEN FORCES: THE EFFECT OF SUPERSENSIBLE INFLUENCES

A book written by the now almost forgotten author Marie Corelli is entitled *The Mighty Atom*. It tells the story of a boy who was brought up on natural scientific explanations only. At the age of 14 he committed suicide. The message is obvious.

There can be no question but that scientific explanations are right and proper in their place but the question remains as to whether they supply the whole truth. What of the unseen dimension in phenomena which we have already pointed out, the spiritual?

Such information as is given here is of vital importance to teachers in Waldorf schools. It influences their attitude and helps them to understand the forces with which they are surrounded, and thus, subconsciously, to open up their children's minds.

With the basic attitude that the world is a manifestation of God and that the living spirit is to be found in all things, stories are told throughout the Waldorf school that have a spiritual background. The emphasis here is on 'told', not 'read'. The telling of stories demands a much greater participation by the teacher, and this reacts favourably on the children. Such stories are a potent means of education since they not only stir the child's imagination but provide spiritual nourishment. Naturally the choice is graded to the age of the child.

We have already alluded to the Old Testament stories given in Class 3. Others taken in the early years are the fairy-tales (Kindergarten and Class 1), legends (2), then Norse and Greek stories (4 and 5) followed by the myths of Ancient India, Ancient Persia and Egypt. All these stories have one characteristic. They portray spiritual truths or human development in picture form.

To illustrate what is meant, let us take a closer look at the so-called fairy-stories. (Actually the designation is a little unfortunate since very few of them have to do with fairies.)

The prince seeking his princess and overcoming obstacles on the way represents the search of the soul for its higher self. The mother figure usually portrays the divine world and the step-mother the earthly. The widow is one separated from the divine. The hero vanquishing the dragon shows the victory of good over evil. Giants represent ancient atavistic forces. The different professions and animals denote distinctive qualities.

Such stories are not only symbolic, they lay a foundation for morality. The good wins.

Some fairy-tales and legends introduce the elemental beings and thus children become acquainted with them. From the Bible stories they learn of the angels. Inspiring material is also to be found in stories of the saints.

In the early years, children have a living connection with objects of nature and thus when the teacher is dealing with these he will use his ingenuity to let them speak or converse with one another as if all are living beings. In this way a feeling for the spirit can be inculcated.

A good example is found in Shelley's poem 'The Cloud': 'I bring fresh showers for the thirsting flowers.' The cloud *speaks*. Another is in Tennyson's 'The Brook': 'I come from haunts of coot and hern.' The brook speaks. An example of conversation is in Emerson's poem 'The Mountain and the Squirrel' where the competitors rail at one another.

Further instances of background influences are provided by history. Constantine has a vision of the cross before battle. Joan of Arc is inspired by St Michael.

In the course of time the subject of spiritual background, like so many others, becomes one for study and discussion. It is a matter for the probing minds of the adolescents.

Such ideas concerning supersensible agencies may be dismissed by the rational thinker as figments of the imagination, but at the same his rational mind might have to admit that on the basis of history there might be some reality. For instance, any research into past or primitive cultures will show a belief in supernatural beings or 'nature spirits'.

In Ancient Egypt it was considered that all nature was permeated by divinity, and hence everything had a divine being within it. But Ancient Greece provides us with perhaps the greatest reference to these elemental spirits since the Greeks experienced beings everywhere. They saw nymphs all around them, dryads in the trees, naiads in the rivers, oreads in the mountains.

Even today in remote districts of the British Isles—and sometimes not so remote—there are people with so-called second sight who are familiar with the nature spirits. Generally, however, in the descent into materialism contact has been lost or maybe the fairies have been driven away, but at some time they must have been visible—the pixies of Cornwall, the hobs of Yorkshire, the boggarts of Lancashire, the little folk and the leprechauns of Ireland. Further afield we learn of the trolls of Norway and the kobolds of Germany.

In fairy-stories we learn about gnomes or dwarfs or elves who are sometimes helpful and sometimes otherwise. In Shakespeare we meet characters like Ariel:

Where the bee sucks, there suck I
In a cowslip's bell I lie
There I couch when owls do cry
On the bat's back I do fly ...

and also the mischievous Puck and other delightful characters in *A Midsummer-Night's Dream*—Peaseblossom, Cobweb, Moth, Mustardseed—all portrayed with a certain amount of poetic licence. Puck speaks:

I must go seek some dewdrops here,
And hang a pearl in every cowslip's ear.

Although there may be fairies or nature spirits assigned to this or that special feature using a variety of names, the usual classification is to consider four types, corresponding to the four elements—earth, water, air and fire. The names of the spirits are gnomes, undines, sylphs and salamanders respectively.

To be aware of them, the special faculty of spiritual vision is necessary; otherwise we must accept the information given to us by one who has this faculty.

*Gnomes.* Gnomes get their name from the Greek word for 'knowing'. They are highly intelligent but it is not a thinking intelligence. They just know—hence their name. They are beings active in the earth, in stone and in metal ores. They maintain the structure of the mineral kingdom. Gnomes are concerned with the root development in plants and give them the power to grow.

One of their characteristics is that they like one another's company and so congregate in the earth in large numbers. *Undines.* Out of the earth the plant comes into the domain of the undines, the water spirits who live in the element where air and water meet. Their name comes from the Latin *unda*, which means a wave or billow. They are active in the union and separation of the substances in the leaves.

*Sylphs.* The sylphs dwell in the warm vibrating currents of air and have an affinity to the birds. They convey light forces to the plant, which affect leaf and flower.

*Salamanders.* A salamander is a sort of lizard who, it was thought at one time, could live in fire. The name has now come to mean a fire spirit. The salamanders are the friends of the insects who visit the flowers. They bring the warmth which the new seeds need to develop. They are active in the ripening of fruit.

The elementals, or nature spirits, are considered the off-spring or the servants of the Hierarchies who were involved in creation. They carry out the will of these higher beings in connection with nature and act as intermediaries. They are active in the forces of the elements, in plant growth and metamorphosis, in animal development and in rhythmic processes such as day and night and the changing seasons.

It is generally recognized today that human activity can destroy nature (pollution, deforestation, nuclear fall-out). The spiritual scientist might express the matter otherwise and say that the nature spirits suffer or are driven out and if they cannot function properly the world of nature deterio-rates.

If the human mind is receptive it can receive inspiration from these beings. It comes in the form of ideas or impulses. Such inspiration may have led to folk remedies, homely medicines and the instinctive wisdom of unsophisticated people.

Just as there is evil in this world, so also there is in supersensible worlds. Among the nature spirits are certain malevolent beings whose influence brings about parasites and poisonous plants. They are nourished by human immorality, lies and wickedness and are even brought into existence through unethical human behaviour.

However, for the most part the elemental beings are well disposed towards human kind, but it pains them if they are neglected and not recognized. Maybe the mischief of sprites, as told in many stories, comes about because humans neglect them and thus arouse their animosity. Their wish is that human beings participate in their world and extend their understanding in general. This is a form of nourishment to them. The story of the Elves and the Shoe-maker illustrates the point.

Stories, legends or poems which concern themselves with the activities of the elemental beings help to convey to children the idea of supersensible forces.

Spiritual science has also much information to give on the diverse nature of angelic beings.

What was said concerning scepticism about the existence of fairies applies equally well to the angelic world. Again, historical evidence exists in abundance.

In all civilizations, ancient or modern, in both primitive and sophisticated peoples, there has existed in various degrees beliefs in higher spiritual beings or agencies who dwell in supersensible realms and have an influence on human beings. Some are beneficial, others malevolent.

If we look at the Bible, we find numerous references to such beings both in the Old and in the New Testaments. Angels in particular are frequently mentioned, usually offering guidance or sustenance. Psalm 91, 11 tells us:

For he shall give his angels charge over thee
To keep thee in all thy ways.
They shall bear thee up in their hands
Lest thou dash thy foot against a stone.

Jacob has a vision of angels ascending and descending a ladder stretched between heaven and earth.

An angel protects Daniel in the lion's den. Angels come to warn the men of Sodom. An angel comes to the aid of Elijah.

Angels announce the birth of Jesus to both Joseph and Mary. Heavenly hosts gather round at his birth. During Christ's temptation in the wilderness 'angels ministered unto him'.

In Luke 16 is the story of Lazarus—the beggar who died and was carried by the angels into Abraham's bosom. (The guardian angel accompanies the soul into the spiritual world.) Beings of higher rank are also mentioned. On the expulsion from Paradise a Cherubim is set to guard the entrance. Isaiah has a vision of the Seraphim above the throne of God.

St Paul speaks of Dominions, Mights, Powers and Principalities. Two archangels are mentioned by name in the

Bible—Michael and Gabriel. In the Apocrypha (14 books that originally formed an appendix to the Old Testament), there is a reference to seven archangels, but only two are named—Raphael and Uriel.

Christian mystical theology speaks of nine choirs of angels. Another name is the Hierarchies.

The different Hierarchies are concerned with different aspects of human and earth development. They themselves are not static figures but are also engaged in a process of evolution. They are therefore at various stages of development. Some achieve a higher rank, some stay behind and the whole array is therefore somewhat complex; the most varied influence flows from them. Some are concerned with the human being, for instance, the angels. These are the nearest to mankind.

In the fairy-story of Snow White and Rose Red, the children go to sleep in a forest, unbeknown to them on the edge of a precipice. In the morning they are aware of a shining white figure standing beside them. It is an angel protecting them. In normal existence, experiences have also been recorded where, at a particular moment of stress, a person feels some sort of protection around him, or some fateful and unexpected event has occurred to rescue him from danger. It is spoken of as divine intervention. Not God but an angel has stepped in.

Every individual has a guardian angel whose task it is to help him transform his lower nature and guide him through earthly life into the spiritual world and again to the next incarnation. The relationship continues until such time as a certain phase in human and earth development is achieved. The guardian angel has a memory of the past and a relationship to the future. He is aware of death and can thus prompt his charge to do something necessary while there is time. The individual receives the message in the form of ideas or impulses. Every night the individual meets his guardian angel who reminds him of his tasks and gives encouragement, although the person may not remember this.

It is important for man's development to foster contact with his angel. One such opportunity is, on going to sleep, to think of being received by the angel and asking for guidance. In general, reverence, morality and altruism are human qualities that will further the contact. The good influence will be felt in the unconscious.

The angels belong to a group known as the Third Hierarchy, of which the other members are the archangels and the archai. The archangels influence peoples and nations, and the archai whole periods of civilizations. The Second Hierarchy (also a group of three) is connected with nature and the life forces of the earth; the First, with earth and the solar system.

In esoteric circles there is a period in history known as the Kali-Yuga and the present is known as the Michael Age. The former refers to a dark age when humanity in general lost conscious connection with the spiritual world. This came to an end in 1899 and the new age opened the door to supersensible experience. Michael, a former archangel, has become the ruling spirit. In the Michael age, which began in 1879, there is a growing desire for spiritual knowledge, for universalism and for an understanding of cosmic Christianity. There is also a movement to overcome nationalism, but the counter-forces are strong.

In the Book of Revelation (12:7) is the story of Michael's fight with the Dragon:

And there was war in heaven: Michael and his angels fought against the dragon; and the dragon fought and his angels. And prevailed not; neither was their place found any more in heaven. And the great dragon was cast out, that old serpent called the Devil, and Satan, which deceiveth the whole world: he was cast out into the earth and his angels were cast out with him.

Thus a direct evil influence is with us, the old dragon, now entrenched in human nature. To counter it, spiritual activity or Michaelic thinking is required. This means attaining a spiritual conception of the world; it means entering into materialistic thinking and transforming it to make natural science a pathway to the spirit. Social justice and morality follow. In an age of freedom, Michael as a presence is ready to assist when asked, and the path towards him is in recognizing the supersensible in the sense world. Then he can inspire.

The beings of the Third Hierarchy are the closest to man, but owing to historical developments their interest in human beings is waning. To receive their inspirations, as with Michael, it is essential for the human being to be spiritually active.

## Forces of Evil

It has already been pointed out that in ancient cultures as well as present ones not only is the existence of angelic beings recorded but also of devils. Once again we can look at our heritage in the Bible and we find endless mention of spirits of adversity under one name or other. Besides the Devil we find Satan, Beelzebub, Belial, the Adversary, the Serpent, the Prince of this World.

Whatever names may be used, spiritual science differentiates between two categories of adversaries. The leader of the one is known as Lucifer and of the other Ahriman. The word Lucifer comes from Latin and means the 'Light Bearer'. Ahriman is to be equated with Satan, a Hebrew word which means the Adversary. When the Bible refers to the Devil, Lucifer is indicated; Satan is Ahriman. Evil spirits could be either. The Devil is responsible for the expulsion from Paradise. Satan is allowed to plague Job. Christ is tempted by both although only the word devil is used. On other occasions the designation evil spirits is used, which Christ casts out; he gives his disciples power over them. St Paul, and other New Testament writers, speak repeatedly of the evil one and his machinations.

Thus opposed to the angelic hosts are the hosts of the forces of evil, which at the present time seem to gather ever-increasing strength. The problem of evil is something we have to face, and it is a human problem that will not be cured by legislation.

An historical perspective that embraces the so-called evil forces is given by spiritual insight as follows.

In the divine plan a being was to be created who would eventually be free, and not be subject to divine guidance. Freedom, however, can only be achieved if there is choice, and progress can only be made by overcoming obstacles. These obstacles were provided by certain members of the Hierarchies (see pp. 93). These beings are able to insinuate themselves into human beings who thereby receive forces that can be turned to either positive or negative use. Lucifer gave humanity the light of self-consciousness, and with that came independence and the possibility of becoming selfish with self-centred passions. With the entry into the physical world came the experience of disease and death.

It must not be thought, however, that the luciferic influence is all evil. Through the luciferic powers the human being has initiative, enthusiasm, freedom and the possibility of forming ideas, but it is when these qualities are unbalanced—when there is, for example, fanaticism—that they become evil.

Traditionally Lucifer is known as the fallen angel whose pride caused the Fall, and it is his aim to usurp God's position and thwart mankind's relationship to God. Today there are many manifestations of luciferic influence. Initiative overdone becomes mania, enthusiasm becomes fanaticism, freedom for self means oppressing others, great ideas become unworkable fantasies. Those living in cloud-cuckoo land, indulging in false mysticism or wallowing in pseudo-occultism are victims of Lucifer.

Lucifer, however, is not the only 'evil one'. At a much earlier stage in history another 'adversary' is mentioned. In the Persian epoch we learn of the struggle between the Power of Light and the Power of Darkness, Ahura-Mazda and Ahriman.

The ahrimanic forces are those most in evidence in present-day western civilization. They manifest in cold, calculated thinking and hardened attitudes, and their influence is to negate all human spiritual striving. Ahriman would like men to believe that only the material world is real. His influence is to be seen in the materialistic concept of the universe, in technology and greed, in distortion of facts, in the use of intelligence without conscience, in considering the human being as a machine.

The two forces assist and mutually support one another. Lucifer led man into the physical world but Ahriman tries to persuade him that this is the only world. This is not a condemnation, since everything has its place. The point is that the human being should not be dominated either by the blandishments of Lucifer or the deceptions of Ahriman. He has to confront the two forces and recognize where their influence is evil.

The battlefield between good and bad is in the human soul. Christ came to give man the power to overcome evil, and by His side is the archangel Michael who, traditionally in Christian thought and legend, is the leader of God's heavenly hosts.

## Influence of the Dead

In the Christian burial service we commit souls to the care of the divine and pray that they will be received.

Through death the excarnated human beings have

become inhabitants of the spiritual world. They are on a journey through the spheres from one incarnation to the next. They are human beings in spirit form whose destiny is still connected to the earth, but they have no direct means of intervention.

It is still possible for them, however, to exert an influence on the people living on the earth. In the same way as the fairies or the angels can whisper a message, so can the departed humans, and it comes to us as a feeling, an idea, an impulse or an inspiration. It is well known that an answer sometimes comes to a problem when we have slept on it. This could well be an example of such communication.

One can even ask the dead for guidance. Before going to sleep one visualizes the friend, relative or the person whose help is being sought, and poses the question. In the forming of the thought or the question a certain technique is essential. It is that, as far as possible, verbs should be used, the activities of objects must be characterized. Nouns are not understood. The question must be imbued with feeling and the relationship must be one of heart and inner interest. The answer may not come at once, and when it does come it may be in a form that is not immediately recognized.

For those engaged in education spiritual science has a special message, which is that if children's parents die young an intimate relationship continues. The parents hover over the children, inspiring them.

We referred earlier to 'divine intervention' by the guardian angel. Such an intervention can also be attributed to an excarnated human being. Conversely, the dead can be helped by the living. If we cultivate memories of our departed friends, send them our love and sympathy, bear in our minds thoughts about spiritual matters, these form a sort of nourishment. In return they stimulate our faculties, inspire us and help us to develop new powers of insight. There are cases where people talk to their departed friends and there are cases where some sort of presence can be felt, which might be a human spirit.

Let it be stated categorically that what is here advocated has absolutely nothing to do with manifestations of departed spirits, mediumistic practices, spiritualistic seances or matters of that sort, which are dependent on trance conditions or depressed states of consciousness.

# 10. NUTRITION AND EDUCATION

In a book which deals with spiritual science and education the reader may be somewhat surprised to find a chapter with the above title. Yet since nothing can be understood in isolation this theme also has a place, not only in what is taught but in the background thinking of the teacher.

At the time of puberty children become more aware of their physical bodies. This is therefore the right time for them to learn something about their own bodily structure, conditions of health and nutrition, and their general relationship to the world. At this age it is a preliminary study, which will be followed in detail in later years and in connection with allied subjects.

Waldorf teaching proceeds from the view of a picture of the harmonious weaving together of the universe to the harmonious working together of the bodily functions. It would of course explain the mechanics and the chemical processes involved in digestion, but would avoid diagrams and pictures at this stage since these tend to give a purely mechanical concept. A description of the interplay of forces, left to the child's imagination, is more in line with a spiritual understanding.

In investigating the process of nutrition, modern scientific thinking has produced an extraordinary wealth of facts concerning proteins, carbohydrates, vitamins and calories—things that can be counted, weighed or measured and manipulated. A balanced, ideal diet can be worked out to suit this or that circumstance. This is typical of a viewpoint that looks upon the human being as a mechanism which is kept working by an adequate supply of fuel.

Things appear a little differently from the aspect of spiritual science.

Analysed, plants are found to contain all sorts of elements—carbon, nitrogen, hydrogen, etc.—and theoretically such substances could be assembled to constitute a very nourishing pill. It would contain the substances needed for bodily activity and the various compounds of the elements—starch, carbohydrates, fats and salts from whatever source. It would be a gourmet's delight and undoubtedly provide a new and exciting item on the menu: 'Chef's speciality, *Pilule à la Mode'*.

But food is not just material substance. It has a living quality, and one has to consider the source of its life. In the words of the Polish mystic Angelus Silesius (1624–77):

Bread does not nourish us.
What feeds us in the bread
Is God's eternal light
His Life and Spirit too.

The nourishment of which we partake has a spiritual quality. And while we are grateful to those engaged in the immediate production of food, it is also appropriate to remember our debt to the agency who made production possible—by saying grace, for instance. Rudolf Steiner gave the following verse which has an extended symbolism:

In the darkness of earth the seed is awakened;
In the light of the air the leaf is quickened;
In the might of the sun the fruit is ripened.

In the shrine of the heart the soul is awakened;
In the light of the world the spirit is quickened;
In the glory of God man's power is ripened.

The chemical and mechanical processes involved in the processes of digestion make a very interesting story, but they are not quite so simple as they appear and certainly not like the picture given of fuel powering a machine.

Food and drink are certainly the main source of human

nourishment. But there are others which are given much less consideration, such as sense impressions and breathing. Think of the satisfaction achieved when viewing a beautiful landscape or listening to a masterpiece of music. Think also of the adverse effects caused by the ugliness of much of our surroundings, or the noise to which we are often subjected. Strange as it may seem, it is not only the body which participates in the process of nutrition but also the soul. For instance, there is an aesthetic side to serving food. The sight of a well-prepared and laid out meal uplifts the soul. So does the smell of fried onions, which also has the effect of making the mouth water. Obnoxious smells can certainly have a dire effect. Anyone who has travelled in a railway carriage full of garlic gastronomes will know what is meant. If raw food is on offer, say apples, there is a joy in handling it, while tasty food brings its own reward. We could also add pleasant or unpleasant company, peace and quiet or being afflicted with endless piped 'music' which, whatever its merits, is intrusive.

These are all matters that have an effect on our metabolic system.

Breathing also provides a form of nourishment. We all require oxygen from the air for our well-being. When it is in short supply or when the air is polluted, our health suffers.

It is common knowledge that undernourishment of the body results in illness and mental deterioration, but undernourishment can occur even if sufficient food has been consumed quantitatively. It is not only that a right balance must be achieved; certain foods or lack of them bring about specific results. This latter point is reinforced when one considers not merely the physical content of food but the forces inherent in it.

The human being is dependent on the plant world for his nourishment, even if he eats plants once removed in the form of meat. His food therefore has a living quality.

Foreign substances are introduced into the body and are

worked on in various ways and transformed. All foodstuffs have to be entirely deprived of their own nature. They have to pass, as it were, through a zero point and then, from the forces which they contain, the human being continually rebuilds his own organism.

There is another factor in human digestion. Whereas the animal seeks out that which it is conditioned to eat, human beings have individual tastes and powers of discrimination. Therefore besides the nutritive value of food it must appeal to the palate. Tastes vary. The French may like snails; the Aborigines, grubs; the Arabs, sheep's eyes; the English, fish and chips.

Each individual human being can consciously choose his food according to taste and requirements, but eating habits are not necessarily in harmony with bodily needs. Responsibility is required in the selection of food, bearing in mind its effects and the fact that it provides the means to sustain the physical vehicle of the human spirit.

It is obvious from the above that matters such as additives, preservatives, refrigeration and canning, as well as methods of cooking, utensils used and production of food, require close consideration.

Some foods we eat raw and some cooked. Cooking food is a help to the digestion and is particularly necessary for those foods which do not digest easily. The point is that raw food requires more effort on the part of the body. But if food is cooked, the body has more strength to expend elsewhere. A balance is necessary so that the digestive system is neither overworked nor allowed to atrophy.

The deleterious effect of alcohol on the mind and on the liver is well known. More subtle effects of other beverages and foodstuffs can be made known through spiritual science.

On the earth, spirit must work through matter and so it is necessary to recognize how it works. Foods can have an effect that is not immediately apparent.

The following remarks by Dr Steiner will give a flavour of the implication. They are a selected sample gleaned from various sources and not necessarily given verbatim. No justification for these statements is made here. They are given in acceptance of Dr Steiner as an authority. Clarification or explanation must be sought in his works themselves or in those who have made a special study of these matters. See *The Dynamics of Nutrition*, by Dr Gerhard Schmidt, and *Nutrition*, by Dr Rudolf Hauschke.

In his first publication on pedagogy, *The Education of the Child*, Rudolf Steiner writes as follows:

The child may be overfed with things that make him lose his healthy instinct completely, but by giving him the right nourishment, the instinct can be so preserved that he always wants what is wholesome for him under the circumstances, even to a glass of water, and turns just as surely from what would do him harm. Spiritual science will be able to indicate all these things in detail, even specifying particular forms of food and nourishment.

Further quotations from Dr Steiner are:

Mother's milk has an awakening influence on the spirit of the child ... Thus nourishment through mother's milk is the first medium of education. [*Study of Man*, Lecture 11]

If you force a child to eat what you think he should eat, it ruins his instinct. [From *Questions on Nourishment*, 2 August 1924]

The perpetual overfeeding of children, stuffing them with eggs and puddings and starchy foods, is one of the things which make children unwilling to learn and incapable of doing so in the early years of their school life.

One should avoid giving tea and coffee to children. Tea

dissipates thoughts. Coffee disposes children to become pedantic. [Statement summarized. From *Discussions with Teachers*, 29 August 1919]

If we observe the embryo of parents who have consumed too many potatoes, we see a more than normal growth of the head and the incarnating soul-spiritual has more difficulty in uniting with it than if the parents had obtained their nourishment from rye and wheat. These are more related to spiritual forces than the potato, which grows in the darkness. [From *Questions on Nourishment*, lecture of 22 September 1923]

If we study these quotations of Dr Steiner's, we see that he is entering a dimension not usually considered, i.e. what is taken into the body as physical nourishment has a spiritual effect. This leads us to the question of the quality of food, which we have already characterized as having a spiritual background.

Dr E. Pfeiffer, a close collaborator of Rudolf Steiner in the agricultural sphere, reports that Dr Steiner gave the following answer to his question as to why people did not have the will to carry out spiritual impulses:

This is a problem of nutrition. Nutrition as it is today does not supply the strength necessary for manifesting the spirit in physical life. A bridge can no longer be built from thinking to will and action. Food plants no longer contain the forces people need for this. [In the preface to Rudolf Steiner's book *Agriculture*]

This statement was made 70 years ago. Since then 'factory' farming has been developed, and there has been more intensive use of fertilizers and pesticides. But also, thankfully, in more recent times there has been a growing interest in organic produce and ecology.

In actual teaching, reference is made throughout the

school to nature and to the life-giving forces. In the younger years stories are told with this background. In Class 3 a particular period is taken on farming and gardening; in story form, the farm is characterized as a living organism. In Classes 6, 7 and 8 children do actual gardening and thus have a direct experience of the divine ordination 'Thou shalt earn thy bread with the sweat of thy brow'. Class 8 has a study period on nutrition.

In the Upper School agricultural studies may well include biodynamic farming, and it may be appropriate here to add a few words about this type of agriculture.

Biodynamic agriculture is based on Dr Steiner's spiritual insight. He considers that the earth is a living organism, subject to cosmic influence, and must be treated as such. Wholesome food does not grow in artificially fertilized soils, nor do vegetables and fruit dosed with pesticides and fungicides produce healthy nourishment. A countryside denuded of trees and hedgerows, in so far as it is farming country, is out of balance.

Biodynamic farms are intended to be self-supporting, i.e. they depend on their own resources for feeding stuffs and manures. There is a balance of animals and crops and regular rotations. Poisonous sprays are anathema. The aim is to produce healthy, fertile soil, and crops grown in such will be sufficiently hardy to withstand pests as well as provide tasty, healthy food.

In biodynamic farming the whole environment is taken into consideration, and that not only includes trees, copses, hedges and animal life but also cosmic influences. Dr Steiner suggested a series of preparations that act on the manure, on the soil and on plants in a way similar to that of homoeopathic medicines on the human body. Some are inserted into compost and manure heaps, others are sprayed on the soil or on the growing plants. They enhance the quality of the product and are natural stimulants.

While a self-contained farm is the ideal, the methods can

be adopted for use in private gardens, nurseries, market gardens and smallholdings.

Anyone who has tasted biodynamic produce will testify to its quality. Even that arch-cynic Bernard Shaw wrote to the donor of a biodynamic loaf (Arnold Freeman): 'At last, something worth-while from a Steinerian.'

Biodynamic produce is now sold under the trade mark 'Demeter'. Further information on the subject is available from: The Bio-Dynamic Agricultural Association, Woodman Lane, Clent, Stourbridge, West Midlands, DY9 9PX.

# 11. THE SIGNIFICANCE OF THE FESTIVALS

Festivals are usually held to celebrate special occasions and many of the established ones have a religious background. Hence they are of some significance in a school that bases itself on spiritual science.

The following notes are for the teacher's consideration.

Europe is the home of Steiner education and here there is a tradition of holding festivities to mark the seasons. Since Europe is in the temperate zone, this means four celebrations—spring, summer, autumn, winter. They will also be celebrated in other parts of the world where conditions are similar. But in view of the fact that Waldorf education is now spreading world-wide, there will no doubt be new developments.

It is a matter of regret that in our urban culture many children have little direct contact with nature. For instance, in England at the beginning of World War II, children were evacuated from the cities to country areas and it was discovered that many of them had never seen a potato grow. They were also disgusted to find that milk came from a cow.

Even when people have access to fields, streams and woods, there is very little real awareness of the significance of the seasons and their relationship to themselves.

Easter is the time for a new bonnet and Easter eggs; Christmas is a time for feasting and drinking, and the almost compulsory practice of giving presents. Midsummer and autumn receive very little attention apart perhaps from the harvest festival in the churches, which relatively few people visit anyway.

Let us, however, consider the background to these festivals.

At one time human beings and nature lived in much closer contact with one another, and the human race had a greater awareness of divine powers. All nature was recognized and appreciated as the deeds of the gods, and the obvious changing face of nature was a marked manifestation of divine power and something to be celebrated.

Such events brought to consciousness the rhythm of the earth, something ordained by divine hand, and thus they provided a spiritual experience.

Celebrations were a sort of worship bringing man closer to the divine, or at least recognizing its existence.

To a great extent a spiritual dimension in life is missing today. But if we are to be 'whole', we need to be aware of these rhythms and the way they are integrated into the whole life of the universe. The earth has to be considered not merely in its physical aspect but as a living organism within a greater context.

The distinguishing feature of living organisms is that they have rhythms, and in the earth-being we can recognize the regular cycle of day and night and that of the seasons. The earth breathes in and out. When it breathes out, it is summer. The flowers blossom, the trees are green, birds and butterflies fill the air and the soul of man expands.

In winter the earth has breathed in, leaving an appearance of death on the surface.

Between the solstices are the equinoxes—spring and autumn—the midpoints of the breathing process.

Northern and southern hemispheres have opposite seasons, which means that on one side of the globe the earth is breathing in and, on the other, breathing out.

Through a suitable celebration the human being can enhance his experience of the changes, not only by bringing them to greater consciousness but by relating them to himself. He can unite something spiritual with sense phenomena.

One obvious factor is the endless round of change yet the

endless recurrence of the same thing. One might ponder the words from the Bible of the preacher, Ecclesiastes 3:1: 'To everything there is a season, and a time to every purpose under the heaven; a time to be born, and a time to die; a time to plant, and a time to pluck up that which is planted.'

The changing of the seasons is an inexorable fact of existence and a source of wonder to one whose mind is not blighted by the incessant stream of distractions. One spring is never like another, nor a summer, nor an autumn, nor a winter; yet we know that one will follow another and in the uncertainties of existence this gives a reassuring feeling that there is some order and stability in the world and a lasting reality.

We live with the seasons. Our feelings and well-being vary with the seasons and the attendant weather. After a dreary winter (here in England) the heart lifts at the sight of the first daffodils and the sound of birdsong; after a hot summer the nip of the first winter frost feels good. We also note that weather has something to do with national characteristics if, for example, we compare the dour Scots with the happy-go-lucky Italians.

Springtime is the period of rejuvenation. It provides confirmation that the life forces have returned after apparent death. The grass turns greener, the trees show their first leaves, the birds are singing, the sky is brighter.

In England one experience of the weather is delightfully expressed in the poem:

April, April,
Laugh thy girlish laughter;
Then the moment after,
Weep thy girlish tears. (William Watson)

The giving of Easter eggs, although the idea is probably overlooked, represents new life. When the Easter bunny brings the eggs there is added symbolism since the rabbit is such a prolific breeder. In an extended symbolism, springtime could be looked upon as the overcoming of materialism.

In summer the soul is drawn out into space. It experiences the warmth and the growth and the abundance of life. We see the multitude of colours in the flowers, the varied shades of green in the trees, the blue vault of heaven and the scudding white clouds. The sun is bright and hot. Nature is at her most exuberant. We enjoy the out-of-doors; the soul wallows in this outward manifestation of divine creation and feels grateful for it.

There is a certain magic in the air, as captured by Shakespeare in his delightful play *A Midsummer Night's Dream* where the humans experience the fairies. It is a time when we can learn the spiritual language of nature, but thinking is difficult. It requires a particular act of will.

The autumn brings the fulfilment of nature's year. It is the time of ripening and of harvest. The trees in their coats of red, brown and yellow radiate an atmosphere of maturity. The hours of daylight are shortened and there is a feeling of contraction in the human soul. Man is referred back to himself. In the experience of harvest he may ponder the question of harvest in the human soul.

Darkness and gloom are the characteristics of winter. We are inclined to shut the door and sit by the fire. The landscape is grey, skies are leaden, the sun is watery and radiates little heat. The forces of death close in. But death is a part of life. The seed has to die in order to grow. We can liken the forces of death to the forces of materialism but, as consciousness develops in contact with the material world, in wintertime there is an enhanced consciousness of self. Man feels within himself.

In spite of the deathlike appearance of the surface of the earth, there is life below, a concentration of forces preparing to burst forth again in due season. Parallel with nature, the human being draws into himself and a resurrection manifests itself in making New Year's resolutions.

Such considerations as the above are applicable whatever the religious background but would obviously need modification in the different climatic zones.

A more difficult problem that has to be addressed has arisen with the spread of Steiner education to non-Christian countries and the influx of ethnic mixtures into the established schools. As explained in a previous chapter, Waldorf schools do not dogmatize; they do not teach *a* religion but they are nevertheless Christian based.

These are matters for a future publication. The following therefore applies only to the schools in the north temperate zone in Christian countries. Friends in the southern hemisphere will have to work out their own connections between the Christian festivals and the seasons.

In the northern hemisphere then, the Christian festivals can be celebrated in parallel with those of nature. Indeed, historically speaking, such festivals have been grafted onto pagan ones.

For instance: the word Easter is derived from the name of a Teutonic goddess of the spring, Eostre. It refers therefore to the season and not originally to the Christian festival. There is a special feature about Easter in that the date varies. It falls on the first Sunday following the first full moon after the vernal equinox. It is determined by connections with the cosmos. The date of the spring equinox is constant (21 March), but the spring weather is certainly not and in England it might even be snowing in March. Nevertheless, Easter is celebrated as the festival of regeneration, a time to consider the idea of 'dying to become'. The Christian has in mind the thought of the death on the cross and the resurrection. Christ entered the etheric sphere of the earth and brought the power by which the human soul can consciously regain the spiritual world.

The summer festival has become St John's Day, the anniversary of the birth of John the Baptist. John was the forerunner. His message was that men should change their attitudes (this is the meaning of repentance) to receive the Christ. The old should be swept away, the soul purified.

The old custom of the midsummer fire, which supposedly cleansed the atmosphere of witches and evil beings and ensured good crops, becomes symbolic. Recalling that John officiated at the entry of the Christ-being into the body of Jesus of Nazareth, it is a time to reflect on the Cosmic Christ.

Michaelmas (29 September) coincides with autumn in the northern hemisphere. From the enjoyment and enrichment received by the experience of space, the human spirit turns inward. The will becomes more active. One has a feeling of inner strength and the urge to act.

Michael sets a good example. He is the archangel who leads the hosts of the Lord. He is Christ's warrior. He fights the dragon. Such a struggle is symbolic of stimulating the will to overcome the lower nature and to strive for inner purity.

In the depths of winter, surrounded by the forces of death, came the child who was to be the bearer of the light. The Bible story says he was born in a stable, legend says in a cave. When candles are lit on the background of a dark fir tree, it is symbolic of the light that shines in the darkness. Greenery brought into the house is a sign of hope. Carols express joy. When presents are given it is a reflection of the love of Christ.

During the 12 holy nights, from 25 December to 6 January, there is a special calm in the atmosphere. The festive season lasts until 6 January, which is now considered the Three Kings Day and it is traditionally the date of the baptism in the Jordan. Thus thoughts are turned again to the great divine Being who entered earthly evolution.

Part of a longer meditation given by Rudolf Steiner is relevant to the Christmas period:

At the turning point of Time,
The Spirit-Light of the World
Entered the stream of Earthly Evolution.
Darkness of Night
Had held its sway;
Day-radiant Light
Poured into the souls of men:
Light that gave warmth
To simple shepherds' hearts.
Light that enlightened
The wise heads of kings.

O Light Divine
O Sun of Christ
Warm Thou our hearts,
Enlighten Thou our heads,
That good may become
What from our hearts we would found
And from our heads direct
With single purpose.

As far as celebrations in school are concerned, the underlying significance will, of course, be in the mind of the teacher. Whatever festivities are arranged will be in accordance with the age of the children.

There is no set form for these festivals. It is a matter left to the genius of the teacher or teachers, but usually they include singing, recitation, stories, a play perhaps, a talk or an address, and may be held by individual classes or the whole school, or both. Younger children will delight in making a seasonal garden table that contains objects belonging to the particular season. There is an abundance of suitable poetry in the English language. At Christmas an advent garden, advent wreath with candles, a Christmas tree and a nativity play are favourites.

## 12.  ESOTERIC DEVELOPMENT AND THE TEACHER

Reference has been made throughout this book to what has been variously termed spiritual perception, enhanced consciousness or knowledge of higher worlds. There follows a short summary here on the path which can be taken to attain such experience.

The interesting thing in the context of Steiner education is that this is the same path that should be followed by every teacher who takes his vocation seriously. He needs to be both doctor and initiate, but that is perhaps too much to expect in the present state of evolution.

The mind of man is so constituted that it is forever reaching outwards and the quest for knowledge is eternal. The philosopher Kant declared that there is a boundary to knowledge beyond which one must have faith. But he was wrong. The boundary of knowledge is only the boundary of the capacity of the mind, but this is capable of infinite extension.

The limits of knowledge are continually being pushed back and the achievements of the mind in investigating the natural world are truly stupendous. But the mind can be attuned to attain even greater knowledge once the existence of a spiritual world is recognized. In fact the many crises of the world today may give rise to the thought that some new thinking and new knowledge is necessary.

We have sense organs with which we investigate the physical world, but to investigate the spiritual other organs are needed. These exist in embryo in every human being but they need to be developed.

In ancient times people lived in a dreamy state of consciousness, directly aware of the creative powers that permeate the world and of the spiritual beings that surrounded them. The course of evolution shows that spiritual vision was gradually lost as far as the general run of mankind was concerned, but another faculty took its place, namely, thinking. The evidence for this lies in the fact that the birth of philosophy took place *c.* 600 BC, in Greece. However, spiritual vision was always open to a select few, those whom we term initiates.

Mankind has evolved and we are now in the age of what some people call the common man. Parallel with the loss of spiritual vision has been the development of self-consciousness. Men and women of today feel themselves as individuals. They do not want to take things on authority. They want to know and to know by virtue of reason.

In many ways science has come to an impasse, and is leading us to Armageddon. Many people feel this and seek solutions. They have an inner perception that all is not well, despite the repeated reassurances by the respective authorities. Natural science has not, and does not, fulfil the longings of the soul. Spiritual science in terms of information may be partially satisfying but personal experience is likely to be much more fulfilling.

Unfortunately the desire for supersensible experience has led to all sorts of aberrations, and hence the drug problem, so-called spiritualism and all sorts of New Age cults. Even journeys into space could be looked upon as a search for extended consciousness, translated into a materialistic medium. The urge for ever greater achievement in sport is symptomatic of extended striving. The spirit is restless.

However, there is a sober path to higher knowledge, open to everyone who is willing to take the necessary steps. It is straightforward but not easy.

Personal guidance and assistance may be helpful if the right person is available, but it is not essential and the way can be found through published literature. There is no need to withdraw from normal life and lead the austere berries-and-water existence of a hermit.

Our western culture has developed the mind in a particular direction. It has cultivated *thinking*, and it is through an enhanced thinking that the way can be opened to the spiritual world in a manner suitable to modern man. Study, concentration, meditation, purity of soul and positive attitudes are basic requirements.

A first essential is a study of what has been given by the masters as spiritual knowledge, and this must be undertaken without preconceptions and misapprehensions. It could be argued that the student is thereby putting himself under undue influence, but he is not asked to believe what he reads or cancel his reasoning faculty. In reality this approach is no different from the study of anything else. It is perfectly logical and it is a method followed by all who would gain expertise. If one is studying mathematics, for instance, it is necessary to learn the concepts, follow the thinking processes which have produced them and acquire the knowledge already attained.

There are specialists in all walks of life. A doctor will have specialist knowledge of one sort; the farmer, of another. With their expert knowledge one could say that both are scientists and both are initiates, albeit they are still concerned with what is available to sense impressions.

But knowledge does not stop there. The would-be spiritual scientist needs to search a little further. He will make progress by learning to observe and experience the meaning of what Goethe expressed in the words 'All things transitory but as symbols are sent'. A concrete example of such an observation is to look at a flower or a tree and appreciate not only its external form and beauty but consider it as the expression of a living being. What forces have brought the plant into existence? What forces sustain it? What is its place in creation? What power awakens the seed? What relationship do plants have to their environment? Many questions can arise but for answers one has ultimately to recognize spirit or one might say the manifestation of God. From this sort of observation feelings are stimulated.

A special exercise in observation is to consider the characteristics of flowers. Why is a red rose the symbol of love? What is the significance behind the name of the dandelion (lion's tooth). All plants have a gesture, and the search for this increases the imaginative faculty. Trees also have different characteristics. One can see the graceful silver birch as a symbol of a dainty lady while the oak presents a picture of a brawny, muscular male.

A further exercise is to observe human beings and, for instance, deduce their temperament from their gait. A light, springy step reveals the sanguine; a measured plod, the phlegmatic.

Thus knowledge is increased by observation. At the same time an attitude has to be cultivated. This is no more than could be expected of a decent, honest, moral person, however difficult it is to live up to an ideal. Nevertheless it is always desirable to strive towards a higher ethical standard.

Actually one could list all the virtues which it is necessary to cultivate—truthfulness, honesty, responsibility, patience, reverence, respect—and all the vices to be avoided, but the recommendations are a little more specific.

Anyone aspiring to attain knowledge of the higher worlds must keep an open mind, be ever ready to learn and be tolerant. That does not mean that he has to suspend his faculty of judgement where it is necessary but that he learns to refrain from pronouncing critical and disparaging views and making egotistical responses. That is to say, he acquires the ability to observe objectively.

He has to overcome egoism, to get out of the habit—if he is afflicted with such—of thinking that his way is the best. He could start from the principle that all characteristics are one-sided and then try to balance his own. He may ask himself 'Am I hot-headed?' If so, I must calm down. 'Do I rush things?' In that case I will act with a little more deliberation. 'Am I too cautious? too reckless? Do I talk too much?' In this way the novice acquires self-knowledge and the purpose of such self-analysis is to produce harmony.

Although requirements are listed in sequence, there is no particular order for their practice. All endeavours are concurrent, but it is obvious that special exercises cannot all be done at the same time.

The student is recommended to practise concentration, to take (for example) a simple everyday object like a pencil and to keep his mind on it. Thought is added to thought about the object without letting the mind wander. Anyone who has attempted this will testify to its difficulty since distracting thoughts continually interrupt.

From this sort of observation advance can be made to more intensive exercises of the imagination. One example is to look at a seed and imagine the whole plant. Another is to consider the sounds as spoken by the human being and consider the significance of each. The student might extend his thoughts to comparing a flower with a human being. In the one he will find an expression of chastity, in the other a mixture of desires.

An exercise of will is to perform a small act regularly at a particular time of the day. The act need not have any particular significance but the will required is considerable.

Feelings have to be controlled. The student learns to accept pain or pleasure with equanimity, to look at himself from the point of view of a third person.

A particular exercise to strengthen the power of the mind is to review the events of the day in backward sequence, even reversing the order of procedure.

Over and above such exercises the aspirant should set aside a few minutes every day to create a period of tranquillity in which he can occupy himself with something entirely different from his daily round. This is meditation, but it is not the sort of meditation where the mind floats away in a cloud of light. Thoughts must be controlled and logical. The mind dwells on a given idea or mental image and retains it in full consciousness. There can be no question of entering a trance condition or hallucinating.

The content of the meditation might be an objective look at incidents in one's own life and their relationship to the world. It might be connected with nature—stones, crystals, plants, animals, and their respective significance in the world order, recognizing the divinity in all things. In particular the content of a meditation could fill the soul with cosmic thoughts as given by the adepts.

Such exercises as the above develop the organs with which the spiritual world can be perceived. But perception in itself is not understanding. We learn the alphabet in order to learn to read but reading is not necessarily understanding. It is the same with the organs of perception. The development of the organs is not the end of the road, merely the beginning.

It should be emphasized that in embarking on the path of knowledge no one should be deflected from his ordinary everyday tasks, nor should he neglect his duties.

The above are indications. For further information the reader is referred to Dr Steiner's book *Knowledge of the Higher Worlds. How is it achieved?*

Such matters as are described above are generally applicable, but the teacher has a specific task—to teach—and a great responsibility. He, of all people, needs not only the knowledge that spiritual science gives but an inward acceptance of such knowledge as well, which also means practising the given exercises. Inner activity means esoteric development and esoteric development provides a revitalizing force which permeates the human being and his work.

Esoteric development will also attract the interest of the

Hierarchies immediately above man, whose interest in mankind, as already stated, is waning. It can, however, be rekindled by human spiritual activity. In particular it is the Third Hierarchy which has concerned itself with mankind in the past, but to attract its attention again the human being has to work on his own soul content. Then the Hierarchy will be in his thoughts and feelings.

It is important to establish this connection so that real spiritual impulses develop and mankind does not get lost in slogans and abstractions.

One thought which will establish a better connection with the angels is that of immortality, but not as it is usually considered by orthodox religion. Immortality in that sense usually means life after death—the reason being that most people do not like the idea of their own finality. But this is a very egoistical thought. Ideas should be turned to pre-birth, to appreciate that this life on earth is a continuation of a previous life in the spiritual world before birth, and a life here on earth before that. In the growing child the spiritual forces become manifest and that applies to all of us.

Another thing to hold the angel's interest is that even in advanced years we should retain joy in new experiences and preserve a youthful zest. This is easier if we have received an education to which we can look back with joy as this provides a rejuvenating experience. Sadly such is not often the case with normal modern education.

At night, in sleep, the human being meets his angel and together they consult on the next day's plans. This is something the human being should consider on waking and he may then feel guided in the right direction.

To achieve inspirations from the archangels, further meditation is necessary on the human being and on a wide selection of spiritual truths, for instance, destiny, karma, spiritual evolution and the advent of the Christ. The archangels have a particular interest in language and are grieved when it is badly used.

The archai are the Time Spirits. Study of the nature of the various civilizations—Egypt/Chaldea, Greece/Rome, the present—means observing the work of the archai, and this brings their interest.

Such activities draw the Hierarchies closer and then their beneficial influence flows down into human thoughts and feelings.

Since the teacher's working material is the human being, the study of man is of paramount importance. In a lecture given on 20 September 1920 (published in *Study of Man*), Rudolf Steiner speaks of three stages of experience:

> The teacher must receive into himself the knowledge of man, meditate upon it and so come to understand it, keep it in mind; then the memory becomes active life. It is not just common memory but rather one that puts forth new inner impulses. This memory comes welling forth from the spiritual life which in turn flows over into our external work. That is the third stage: meditative comprehension is followed by active, creative recollection which is at the same time responsiveness to what emanates from the spiritual world.

Furthermore, the responsible teacher will reflect meditatively on the particular children he teaches, even to the extent of asking the assistance of their guardian angel. He will ask the beings of the Third hierarchy, those particularly concerned with the human race, for help in his work.

In Chapter 1 reference was made to the founding of Steiner education under divine guidance. Such guidance is always available, but since in the course of history man has achieved a certain independence from the gods, angelic beings do not impose. Their inspiration and assistance will flow in proportion to the teacher's spiritual development. In particular the beings of the Third Hierarchy stand in readiness to support humanity.

To foster the connection between teachers and the Third

Hierarchy Rudolf Steiner gave information which could be considered a kind of prayer or meditation. The actual words are available only to college members but the following is the gist of its contents.

He spoke of the teacher's guardian angel who stands behind him, giving strength and the power of imagination. As a collective body, working together, the college attracts the attention of the next rank, the archangels, who help unite its members and give courage and inspiration. When united in common striving, the archai, in particular the Spirit of the Times (Michael), gives to the group the light of wisdom and the creative forces of intuition.

# APPENDIX

The following are very short summaries of themes mentioned in the text but which have little direct connection with education. They are included here so that readers may have some inkling of how Anthroposophy views these matters.

## The Spiritual-scientific View of Evolution

There are two stories of creation apart from the myths of primitive peoples. One is the Big Bang theory, the other is expressed in the first words of the Bible.

Spiritual science describes the creation as follows.

The earth and the solar system came into being as a result of divine activity. It was the decision of high ranking spiritual beings—the Hierarchies, or God if the term is preferred—to create new worlds and a human race. They gave of their substance, and creation took place in stages. Through a series of densifications or contractions, the present earth was created. The stages are usually referred to as warmth, gas, liquid and solid, but apart from solid the designation can only be approximate. One might say that these elements were of the nature of warmth, gas, etc., or that they were prototypes or spiritual ancestors. Even solid was not at first solid as we now understand the term. Sun, moon and planets were left in the periphery, manifesting as heavenly bodies but in reality they are centres of forces or homes of beings radiating their forces. Beyond the solar system are the stars and the constellations of the zodiac, which are also centres of radiating forces and homes of other beings. The human being existed in spirit form as an idea of the gods.

At each stage spiritual beings introduced something new. Transformations and interactions took place and the eventual result was the formation of the four kingdoms of nature on earth. All these took place before the advent of time as we know it.

The story of creation in Genesis refers to a particular stage in the development that ends in the final densification of the physical earth. The 'Beginning' is the beginning of this stage. The first 'days' describe the recapitulation of former conditions and must still be considered as non-material happenings. Then comes the actual creation of the earth, although not yet solid, and all belonging thereto. And God said: 'Let there be lights in the firmament of heaven to divide the day from the night and let them be for signs, and for seasons and for days and for years.' Time begins. The Hierarchies are still engaged in forming a suitable vehicle for the human spirit. The animal forms and the subsequent animals represent what was unsuitable. The human being does not yet exist in the physical. When we are told that God made man on the sixth day the reference is to a staging post, a stage of development. 'Male and female' created he them is a mistranslation. It should be male/female, i.e. hermaphrodites.

We come to a period known as Lemuria, after the name of a continent supposedly situated between Africa and Australia, an area now covered by the Indian Ocean. The atmosphere was something between air and water but contained forces of life; the land was something between liquid and solid and it was hot and volcanic.

At the beginning of this period earth and moon were one, but due to the intervention of higher beings the moon was expelled and with it certain forces of hardening which would have had a detrimental effect on earth's development. Some solidification began to take place, and it is from this time that one can begin to speak of geological formations.

The human being still lived in Paradise, i.e. the spiritual world, but he was being prepared to enter physical existence.

The Bible describes a second creation of man: 'And the Lord God formed man of the dust of the ground and breathed into his nostrils the breath of life; and man became a living soul.'

What we have here is a statement that the human being has received both earthly and heavenly forces. The dust is of earth; with the divine breath man's spirit is incorporated into the vehicles already prepared for it.

Parallel with the hardening of the earth's crust, a move towards the development of a physical human form took place. At this stage it was, however, still very malleable and open to all sorts of influences, including those of the forces within the soul that could still mould the plastic physical form. Some human beings became more attuned to earthly conditions than others, who remained more susceptible to spiritual influences. The end result of this was the development of the two sexes.

However, evolution is not only concerned with human beings but also with the Hierarchies. Angels and archangels are also in a state of development. It happens that higher beings, as well as lower ones like ourselves, fall behind, in which case their influence has an apparently negative effect. The word 'apparent' is used here advisedly since, in the context of evolution, negative effects can have a positive result. Such beings are those known as luciferic. They had become self-willed and sought for their own ends to influence humans. They are represented by the serpent. They awakened man's senses—'opened his eyes' in the Paradise story—and by becoming increasingly self-conscious in the sense world the human being recognized good and evil. His expulsion from Paradise relates to his loss of spiritual vision (banished by God), to pursue his life in the material world.

Lemuria, as a continent, eventually disappeared beneath

the seas, but certain groups of peoples had emigrated to an area that was becoming more stable. This was Atlantis, now covered by the Atlantic Ocean. Here various settlements were made in different parts and each developed in its own way, the result of which was the formation of different races. If one can speak of civilization, it was a civilization very unlike our own. The state of human consciousness was entirely different. Men then had no power of logical thought but did possess a phenomenal memory. Soul still influenced the bodily form. Humans had magical powers which could influence natural happenings. These powers were eventually used to evil effect, with the result that the mist-atmosphere which covered the continent dispersed, resulting in a flood and the disappearance of the land. (Developments in post-Atlantis were described in Chapter 7.)

## Christianity: The Cosmic View

In his letter to the Corinthians, St Paul writes:

> For as the body is one, and hath many members, and all the members of that one body, being many are one body; so also is Christ. For by one spirit we are all baptized into one body, whether we are Jews or Gentiles, whether we be bound or free; and have been all made to drink into one spirit. [1 Corinthians 12:12.]

The above infers that there is only one humanity. Different peoples may have different concepts and capacities but, unlike the animals of which there are multitudes of species, human beings are united in a common humanity. The one spirit of which Paul speaks is the Christ who is beyond all separate religions, churches or sects. He came for all mankind irrespective of race, nation, colour or any other distinction.

All religions have something to offer, but Christianity is unique in its cosmic dimension.

There was a time when humanity had no need of religion, or we could say that religion did not exist.

In Chapter 7 we considered the various cultural epochs and saw how in these succeeding civilizations we can trace the change and development of human consciousness. From an awareness of the spiritual world and vague consciousness of the physical, the path leads to an inversion, a very strong awareness of the physical and an almost total unconsciousness of the spiritual. At the same time the feeling for self, for independence, grows. Before these times, human minds were even more attuned to the spirit and enjoyed direct perception and divine guidance. Only when direct contact fades does religion develop. The word 'religion' means 'to re-unite', and its function is to form a bridge between the spiritual and the physical world.

In the Ancient Indian period people recognized a divine power in the spiritual sphere of the sun which they called Brahma. The spiritual influence that emanated from this power was known as Vishna Karman, a name which means the Word.

From Persia we have the legends of Zarathustra and his conversations with Ahura-Mazda, the wise spirit who lived in the aura of the sun. From this spirit Zarathustra received his inspiration. The Egyptians also had a sun god, Ra, known as the Shining One. On earth Ra's representative was Osiris. The Egyptian initiates experienced spiritual forces coming from the sun. The heretical Pharaoh Akhenaton asserted that the great being who had lived in the sun-sphere was no longer there.

In Greece there was a dual concept of the sun. The physical sun was termed Helios, but the Greeks also felt the presence of a sun god around them. He was called Phoebus Apollo. The Roman legions venerated Mithras, also a sun god.

In this sequence we note that a god identified with the spiritual essence of the sun is coming nearer to the earth.

Moses had an experience of a god in the elements, in a burning bush. 'And God said unto Moses "I am the I am" and he said: Thus shalt thou say unto the children of Israel—I AM hath sent me unto you' (Exodus 3:14).

At the baptism in the Jordan this God incarnated into a human body. The distinction must be made clear between the terms Jesus of Nazareth and Jesus Christ. The former was a gifted, highly evolved human being. At the age of 30 the ego of this human being yielded its physical, etheric and astral bodies to the divine being whom we call Christ, the Greek word for the 'Anointed One'. It was of course a unique event and had required special preparation over a long period of time. The Hebrew people were selected and given the task of providing a suitable vehicle into which a god could incarnate. This was the reason why the Jews had to retain the purity of blood and submit to strict laws. With the coming of Christ the Jewish mission was fulfilled.

The incarnation of Christ was destined to take place at this point of time in accordance with the path of evolution of mankind.

We have called attention to the fact that in the sequence of civilizations, awareness of the spiritual worlds (i.e. God or the divine) receded. The nadir was reached in the Roman world, when the divine connection could have been lost altogether. This crisis was averted by the advent of Christ, by the fact that men could actually experience a God in the flesh.

The coming of Christ had another result. Christ actually brought a power—one could describe it as a spiritual aura which diffused into the earth—and this power gave man the conscious experience of his ego, the I AM. The approach of this Christ power, the I AM, is what is indicated in the story of Moses and the burning bush.

With the strength of the ego, man now had the possibility

of steering a path through the two opposing forces of evil. He now had the power through his own ego forces of dealing with the world of matter and penetrating it to find the spiritual background. That is to say he could now awaken by his own effort those powers by which he could again become aware of the spiritual world, but this time consciously. This is what St Paul means when he says: 'Not I but Christ in me.'

It is not an immediate development but one which is beginning to mature at the present time.

In earlier ages the divine powers had been experienced as arising from without. Now there is an experience of the God within. There was a foreshadowing of this in the experience of Elijah when the Lord did not speak to him from the wind, or the earthquake or the fire, but he heard a still small voice. Another example comes from Greece. The Furies are the avenging spirits attacking from without, but in the course of time the inner voice of conscience takes their place. Christianity itself is concerned with the God within.

It is now generally acknowledged that the Gospels are not exact records. They contain descriptions of events, stories and moral guidance, but the essence of Christ's teaching could be summarized in one of his sayings: 'Seek ye first the Kingdom of God.' The Kingdom of God is the spiritual world. Modern spiritual science gives information on spiritual matters as has been detailed in the previous chapters. The path to the spiritual world as advocated in the Gospels is by purification of the soul, prayer (which we should now term meditation), and love.

The good spirits will help us if we are sufficiently worthy. It is even possible to have direct experience of the Christ. This is attainable through the development of higher faculties of spiritual perception, since Christ is now to be found in the etheric aura of the earth. St Paul (Saul) on his way to Damascus was the first person to experience the Christ in this way. This is the so-called Second Coming, but the Second-Coming is a misnomer. The original Greek speaks of a 'presence', and the 'presence' is to be experienced by those whose faculties are sufficiently enhanced.

In St Luke 21:25 we read the following:

And there shall be signs in the sun, and in the moon, and in the stars; and upon the earth distress of nations with perplexity; the sea and the waves roaring; men's hearts failing them for fear, and for looking after those things which are coming on the earth; for the powers of heaven shall be shaken and then shall they see the Son of Man coming in a cloud with power and great glory. And when these things come to pass, then look up and lift up your heads; for your redemption groweth nigh.

The passage could well apply to modern times with its problems of pollution, ecology, social unrest, wars and rumours of wars, and at the same time the realization of the necessity for spiritual enlightenment.

# A NOTE ON RUDOLF STEINER

In this book many references have been made to unseen forces, to spiritual powers, which affect all our lives. It is obvious in the case of Rudolf Steiner that some great spiritual agency, some superhuman power, stood behind him. Only by accepting this is it possible to comprehend the immensity of the knowledge which he disseminated and the multitude of activities in which he engaged.

For the most part we mere mortals are not conscious of spiritual influences, but this does not apply to Rudolf Steiner who had the faculty of direct contact with the spiritual world.

Look where you will, he provides enlightenment and positive suggestions.

In the first place we should have to cite his expositions of spiritual science, or Anthroposophy, of which some chapters of the present book are summaries.

Secondly are the numerous impulses which he gave in certain spheres of practical life. One could mention Waldorf education, biodynamic agriculture, anthroposophical medical practice, Weleda (manufacturers of anthroposophical medicines, etc.), and the Threefold Social Order.

Thirdly is a new direction in art—drama, painting, sculpture, architecture, and the new art of movement which he himself created, eurythmy.

Fourthly, one has to recognize Rudolf Steiner as a creative artist. He designed the imposing structure known as the Goetheanum in Switzerland, which is now the world centre of his work. He designed and personally worked on a huge wooden statue which represents Christ between Lucifer and Ahriman. He wrote plays depicting in dramatic form the message of Anthroposophy.

Perhaps one should also mention his work as counsellor since an unending stream of individuals came to him for personal advice.

Some people may refer to Dr Steiner as a mystic or a visionary and to some extent this is justified. He was a mystic in the sense that the spiritual world was open to him but he was also a mystic with his feet firmly on the ground.

Several biographies of Rudolf Steiner exist to which the reader is referred. The following is but a brief outline of his life and work.

Rudolf Steiner (1861–1925) was Austrian by birth but his birthplace, Kraljevic, is now in Croatia.

After attending village schools he studied the official science course at college but at the same time taught himself the classics. Eventually he gained a degree as Doctor of Philosophy.

At the age of 21 he was invited to edit an edition of Goethe's scientific writings and he became a recognized authority on these matters.

In 1890 he took up residence in Weimar, the then cultural centre of Germany, where he made the acquaintance of the intellectuals of the day and engaged in literary work. Seven years later he moved to Berlin to edit the *Magazin für Literatur*. At the same time he joined the staff of a working men's college.

He had already begun to express certain of his ideas in writing and in 1894 his book *The Philosophy of Spiritual Activity* was published. This was followed by *Christianity as Mystical Fact* (1902), *Theosophy* (in the sense of divine wisdom) (1904), *Knowledge of the Higher Worlds* (1904) and *Occult Science, An Outline* (1910).

At about the turn of the century he felt himself sufficiently mature to speak on esoteric matters. For a time he was associated with the Theosophical Society but eventually found some of their views unacceptable and a number of his special adherents decided that a new society should be formed. This was the beginning of the Anthroposophical Society, of which Dr Steiner became president at a later stage.

The necessity for a geographical centre led to the building of the Goetheanum in Dornach, Switzerland.

Rudolf Steiner now lectured extensively all over Europe as well as in Dornach. Many of these lectures or lecture cycles were given in response to requests, often from experts in their own fields, such as farmers, doctors, teachers, actors and ministers of religion.

As an example of his activity, in 1911 (the year was chosen because it is the year of the author's birth) Rudolf Steiner visited some 40 cities and gave nearly 200 lectures. Shortly before his death he was averaging 400 lectures a year which were not repeats but had special themes such as social problems, natural science, health, illness, music, history, the arts and education, in addition to general Anthroposophy. At the same time of course he was engaged with society matters, the building of the Goetheanum and a thousand and one other things besides.

His literary and lecturing output was prodigious. His lectures are now printed in book form and together with the written books his collected works (in German) runs to 350 volumes. In German alone 200,000 of his books are sold annually while translations of at least some of them exist in all European languages as well as in Hebrew, Japanese, Hindi and Turkish.

Rudolf Steiner was convinced that in this materialistic age a new understanding of spiritual matters was a vital necessity for the future welfare of mankind. He felt himself called upon to provide this new insight.

## Books about Rudolf Steiner

Rudolf Steiner, *The Story of my Life*, Rudolf Steiner Press.

Johannes Hemleben, *Rudolf Steiner — A Documentary Biography*, Henry Goulden.

Roy Wilkinson, *Rudolf Steiner — Aspects of his World View*, Temple Lodge Publishing.

Gilbert Childs, *Rudolf Steiner: His Life and Work*, Floris Books.

Stewart C. Easton, *Rudolf Steiner: Herald of a New Epoch*, Anthroposophic Press.

# BIBLIOGRAPHY

In compiling this book reference has also been made to the following by Rudolf Steiner. Except where otherwise mentioned, all are available from Rudolf Steiner Press (London) or Anthroposophic Press (New York).

*Macrocosm and Microcosm.*
*The Being of Man and his Future Evolution.*
*Man as Hieroglyph of the Universe.*
*An Occult Physiology.*
*Supersensible Physiology and Balance in Teaching,* lectures of 21/9/20 and 22/9/20.
*The Gospel of St John.*
*Universe, Earth and Man.*
*Cosmic Memory,* Rudolf Steiner Publications, Englewood, USA.
*Reincarnation and Immortality,* Rudolf Steiner Publications, Englewood, USA.
*Anthroposophy—An Introduction.*
*Manifestations of Karma.*
*Reincarnation and Karma.*
*Occult History.*
*Man's Being, his Destiny and World-Evolution.*
*Supersensible Man.*
*The Inner Nature of Man.*
*Planetary Spheres and Their Influence on Man's Life on Earth and in the Spiritual Worlds.*
*Man as Symphony of the Creative Word.*
*The Influence of Spiritual Beings upon Man.*
*The Mission of Folk Souls.*
*The Spiritual Hierarchies.*
*The Spiritual Guidance of Mankind.*
*The Influences of Lucifer and Ahriman.*
*The Dead are with Us.*
*Agriculture* (edited by E. Pfeiffer)
*The Cycle of the Year*
*The Festivals and their Meaning*

## Other Authors

Gerhard Schmidt, *The Dynamics of Nutrition*, Bio-Dynamic Literature, Wyoming, USA.

Rudolf Hauschke, *Nutrition*, Stuart and Watkins, London.

Lawrence Edwards, *The Vortex of Life*, Floris Books, Edinburgh.

Alfred Schütze, *The Enigma of Evil*, Floris Books, Edinburgh.

Sue Fitzjohn, Minda Weston, Judy Large, *Festivals Together*, Hawthorn Press.

Diana Carey, Judy Large, *Festivals, Family and Food*, Hawthorn Press.

Adrian Anderson, *Living a Spiritual Year*, Threshold Publishing, Australia. (An interesting book dealing with seasonal festivals in the northern and southern hemispheres.)

## Fundamental Works on Anthroposophy by Rudolf Steiner.

*Occult Science, An Outline.*
*Theosophy* (to be understood in the sense of 'divine wisdom').
*Knowledge of the Higher Worlds. How is it Achieved?* Also published as *How to Know Higher Worlds.*
*Theosophy of the Rosicrucian.*

For a philosophical approach to spiritual science:

*The Philosophy of Spiritual Activity.* Also published as *Intuitive Thinking as a Spiritual Path.*

On education, Rudolf Steiner gave many lecture courses, to many different audiences, in different places, at different times. A certain amount of repetition is therefore to be expected. The main compilations of lectures are:

*Modern Values in Education*
*A Modern Art of Education*
*The Study of Man*
*Practical Advice to Teachers*
*The Spiritual Ground of Education*

*The Kingdom of Childhood*
*The Essentials of Education*
*The Roots of Education*
*Soul Economy and Waldorf Education*
*Discussions with Teachers*

One written work by Steiner is: *The Education of the Child in the Light of Anthroposophy.*

## General Introductions to Rudolf Steiner Education

L.F. Edmunds, *Rudolf Steiner Education,* Rudolf Steiner Press.
Roy Wilkinson, *Commonsense Schooling* Rudolf Steiner College Press.
Roy Wilkinson, *Rudolf Steiner on Education,* Hawthorn Press.
Roy Wilkinson, *Questions and Answers on Rudolf Steiner Education* Rudolf Steiner College Press.

## Educational Guides/Resource Books by Roy Wilkinson

The list below covers the subjects up to age 14. All the books are now published by the Rudolf Steiner College Press, California.

*The Curriculum of the Rudolf Steiner School*
*Teaching English*
*Teaching Mathematics*
*Teaching Geography*
*Practical Activities* (Farming, Gardening, Housebuilding)
*Man and Animal*
*Plant Study/Geology*
*Physical Sciences* I (Physics)
*Physical Sciences* II (Chemistry)
*Nutrition/Health/Anthropology*
*History: The Ancient Civilizations*
*History: From the Renaissance to the Second World War*

## *Some Other Books by Roy Wilkinson*

(All published by Rudolf Steiner College Press, California.)

*Miscellany*—original poems and plays
*Old Testament Stories*—retold
*Commentary on the Old Testament Stories*
*The Interpretation of Fairy Tales*
*The Significance of the Norse Stories*
*Plays for Puppets*
*The Origin and Development of Language* (Hawthorn Press)
*The Temperaments in Education*

# YOUR REINCARNATING CHILD
*Dr Gilbert Childs & Sylvia Childs*

'One of the main purposes of this book', write the authors, 'is to demonstrate that human beings are primarily of spiritual nature, and only secondarily of bodily nature'. They explain how these two natures complement each other in the processes of maturation and development from the period before birth, or incarnation, to maturity.

Mainstream educational policies and practises can result in children being pushed prematurely towards adulthood, before having had a chance truly to experience childhood. But, as the authors demonstrate, an understanding of the nature of the human being as body, soul and spirit indicates that every child should be allowed to grow slowly into the world.

The primary contention of this book is that, as a spiritual being, each one of us lives beyond death, eventually returning to earth in a new human body. With this knowledge in mind, the authors give much sound practical advice as to how parents and those around each child can help it properly to incarnate and grow into a healthy and responsible human being.

ISBN 1 85584 037 5; Sophia Books; 192pp; £9.95

# UNDERSTAND YOUR TEMPERAMENT!
## *Dr Gilbert Childs*

We are all interested in learning how better to understand ourselves and others, and this book is a most refreshing treatment of the ancient doctrine of the four temperaments, namely *choleric, sanguine, phlegmatic* and *melancholic*. Dr Childs demonstrates just how viable this classic concept is in modern times, and just how we are all the same—yet different! Moreover, he shows us how to recognize the temperaments in ourselves and others, and appreciate their working in our behaviour, and hence become better integrated as individuals.

The book is conversational in tone, while investigating in considerable depth the origins and manifestations of the temperaments in terms of recent thinking, in both their psychological and physiological aspects. There are fascinating discussions of the relationships between adults of various temperaments and matters of compatibility in partnership, family, and workplace situations, all liberally spiced with amusing examples of likely scenarios as appropriate. There is also a section dealing with the temperaments of children, which includes helpful advice on how to help them in terms of attributes and behaviour.

The book ends with an examination of orthodox scientific theories concerning the origins of the *three* bodily types, and the seemingly impossible question of relating these to the *four* temperaments. Dr Childs posits a likely solution to the arithmetical problem: four into three does not 'go'!

This book is highly recommended reading for everyone interested in improving interpersonal relationships—**and that includes YOU!**

ISBN 1 85584 025 1; Sophia Books; 160pp; £9.95